Tracy Porter's
Inspired Gatherings

These are my thoughts this is my language

OTHER BOOKS BY TRACY PORTER

Tracy Porter's Dreams from Home

Woven in Sunlight ~ A Garden Companion

Returning Home ~ The Poetics of Whim and Fancy

Dream with Your Eyes Open

LITTLE BOOKS

Gentle Influences: The Spirited Ties of Sisters

The Journey Within: A Book of Hope and Renewal

Celebrating Babies

Tracy Porter's
Inspired Gatherings

WRITTEN AND CREATED WITH DEBORAH HERNANDEZ AND SARAH WILLETT
PHOTOGRAPHY BY KATY ROWE AND DALE STENTEN

These are my thoughts this is my language

Andrews McMeel Publishing

Kansas City

www.andrewsmcmeel.com

99 00 01 02 03 TWP 10 9 8 7 6 5 4 3 2 1

Library of Congress Cataloging-in-Publication Data
Porter, Tracy.
        Tracy porter's inspired gatherings / written and created by Deborah Hernandez and Sarah Willett : photography by Katy Rowe and Dale Stenten.
        p. cm.
    ISBN 0-7407-0046-4
    1. Entertaining. I. Hernandez, Deborah. II. Sarah Willett. III. Title. IV. Title: Inspired gatherings
    TX731 .P665 1999
    642'.4—dc21   99-22162
                                        CIP

ATTENTION: SCHOOLS AND BUSINESSES

Andrews McMeel books are available at quantity discounts with bulk purchase for educational, business, or sales promotional use. For information, please write to: Special Sales Department, Andrews McMeel Publishing, 4520 Main Street, Kansas City, Missouri 64111.

Thank You, Thank You, Darlings!

For dreaming with your rose-colored glasses on!

xoxo   T.

Chris Schillig	Dave and Annette Schaberg
Tom Thornton	Annie Porter
John McMeel	John Castino
Kathy Andrews	Angie Daye
Polly Blair	Maura Koutoujian
Dorothy O'Brien	Todd Doherty
Julie Herren	Robyn Schaberg
Deb (Poncho) Hernandez	Leslee, Gary, and Elsa Hannabarger
Sarah Willett	Darlene and Bob Copeland
Katy Rowe and Dale Stenten	The entire Andrews McMeel staff
John Porter	Grandma Schaberg—For being our biggest fan
Christine Phillips	Henry's (The Store)
Jodie Ferguson	To our licensees—We couldn't do it without you!
Trish Krumbein	The city of Princeton and surrounding communities— We love it here.
Jean Meyer	
Jean Koerner	

For John, who every day feeds my soul and brings laughter to every occasion.

For our parents, Margo and Paul, John and Kathryn, Dave and Annette for creating pure magic at every gathering with family and friends . . . how can one not be inspired by the examples you set.

For the delicious team of people that I am surrounded by every day. You are my friends and my family, and you are my light.

XOXO

Contents

Contradiction is a healthy way to live—it will bring balance. You can even see it in this place setting, in contrasts of texture, color, pattern, and all those layers. We brought the indoors out by using a velvet leopard scarf as an elegant table runner and dipping into my jewelry box for an antique necklace that holds rolled napkins. Pretty foil-wrapped candies sprinkled on the table contradict the weatherworn roughness of this wrought iron table and chair set. Bringing all of it together, definitely tickles my eclectic side.

CHAPTER 1

An Opera of Chaos

"Life is not a dress rehearsal." Whoever said that first, I love them. When I am immersed in a fantasy project like creating this book, I have one objective: You, my readers, must be so deliciously inspired that you savor each page. I hope this book will be the last thing you see before you float off into your dreams. To help you get to the place where you're that dazzled, we have to give you some magic—the kind of magic you can really play with that we call "attainable fantasy." In the best scenario, the journey toward magical fantasy is the way we try to live our lives, gather with friends, and share with our families. And for all of my fascination with the creative process and imagination, they really don't compare with the beauty of living and sharing with friends and family. Unlike a fantasy, *the entertaining experience is filled with love and emotion—things we are only lucky enough to know in the here and now of real life.*

So if you take real-life gatherings and sprinkle them with some sugar, what do you get? Hopefully, this book! Attainable fantasy— try it on and see how it fits.

I do have one fear about creating this kind of book—I don't want you to get the wrong impression about us. We don't live every single minute of our lives like something out of this book. Sure, we have our fantasy days, and, like you, we have many moments filled with pure magic. But our surroundings are not perfectly glittered and tied in ribbons every day.

Just because on some days I want to add something a little special to my table setting doesn't mean that I've become a slave to those settings and have to make each table better than the last. Listen, I like to strive, and I love to have my fun, but like you, I have days when I don't want to deal with any of it. Many nights, my husband John and I park it in front of the television with friends, feet up and a carry-out pizza in hand. Other occasions inspire me to push the limit, create some over-the-top centerpiece, and serve dinner by the course. That's my reality; I try to pick my battles.

I have a theory about why people get so intimidated about entertaining. It's because they're not focusing on the good stuff, too busy worrying about the additional workload instead of considering the way their special details will affect the entertaining experience for everyone, themselves included.

I tend to view situations that seem overwhelming as an opportunity to create. When I think of entertaining, I focus first on incorporating something I love into the event. Many people get bogged down with thoughts about cleaning the house, polishing the silver,

When I set up a room, my approach is to let it evolve.
Like most things in my life, home is also a work in progress.

running for groceries, preparing the food, and so on. If I start out thinking about what will be special about the gathering, like finding inspiration for a centerpiece or making the invitations, it gets me really excited about the whole process of entertaining.

Filling the space with flowers, lighting the candles, and selecting the music are the rituals that keep me calm right before the chaos of one of our get-togethers. I imagine myself as the director of a play, orchestrating the stage secretly from behind the scenes, knowing full well that once the cast of characters shows up, all hell will undoubtedly break loose. Our gatherings are seldom reserved. I like an evening filled with hilarity and laughter better than one where poise, perfect table manners, and polite restraint are required. We try to surround ourselves with people who love a good cocktail, have a voracious appetite for fine food, and let the conversation become wicked good fun.

It's important to know that you don't need any special qualifications to be a good host to your friends and family. Maybe you just feel like I do—excited and passionate about getting everyone together. By trade, I'm not a caterer or a decorator—I consider myself to be an explorer  and an experimenter; my approach to entertaining evolves in the same way my life does. This book is not a foolproof plan for successful entertaining. It's more about sharing my experiences with you. What you do with that inspiration is up to you.

I don't reinvent the wheel when I invite people over. Instead, I keep adding to my stash of resources so each time it gets a little easier. If I encourage you to look in your cupboards and use what you have, it's only because I've tried this myself when I'm pressed for time or can't spend the money for something new. I want to encourage you to think about entertaining in a new way, to open your mind to changing some of the traditions. What I'm about is the mix, not the match. As a designer, I'm constantly

Give yourself more credit. Allow yourself the freedom to try it all on. After all, more is more.

Before I jump into an event or gathering, I ask myself several questions:

Is there enough seating for guests? Where and how will food be served~at the table? buffet style? How many guests? What's the menu? How will I be inspired? Shall I call or send invitations? Dress~cool and casual, or feathered and fabulous?

trying exercises that will expand my creative process. Inspiration exists all around us, I hope you let it enhance your every day.

Your lifestyle is just that—yours. You needn't live up to anyone's expectations but your own. It's about finding your own voice. For me, there is an added element of excitement in knowing that the voice I find today will not necessarily be the same tomorrow. Sometimes you've gotta have what you've gotta have for this moment—I definitely surrender to this mantra time and time again. Change is healthy.

I like the freedom of knowing that I don't have to do and be all things when I entertain. Sometimes I just want to take a piece of somebody's world, like the color of a flower in a friend's garden, and let it inspire my next centerpiece. Perhaps your gatherings can help inspire friends to add creativity to their lives. You might not realize it, but you are actually helping to push them out of their nest. That flight is the most beautiful of any you will see.

Thinking creatively doesn't have to cost more money~it usually costs less. Allow yourself the luxury of several free thoughts a day.

Freedom of expression brings experiences that are truly rich. It's about expanding and digging, embracing the idea of change. I like the idea that life is a gift we are meant to experiment with. Every day we can try on something new, relieve ourselves of structure. To me, structure feels heavy and confining, although I can respect that it has its place. For just a moment, think about what you need right now—freedom or a firm guideline—and follow your heart.

There is no right way to use this book, and there really isn't a wrong way to use it, either. If it strikes a chord with you or inspires you to try something in a new way, then I will have achieved my goal.

In many events captured in this book, I've shown examples of how to alter the use or function of something small. A decorated shoe box becomes an individual picnic basket; a book is used as a coaster. Rice is even used as wrapping paper! Like I've said, the possibilities are endless.

Style knows no boundaries

Small Rooms

If it's an intimate gathering, sometimes tight quarters add to the coziness of the evening. Some of our most emotionally charged evenings have been spent with friends in a small room lit by candles.

- Try low-watt bulbs in all of your lamps to create a more sensuous atmosphere.
- Save space by forfeiting the formal setting of a table and casually share hors d'oeuvres with friends.

Living Room

We tend to use it when we're with really close friends or family and we just want to be comfy. Overstuffed sofas, a coffee table where everyone puts their feet up makes for a "hey, does anyone mind if we just order carryout and put the game on?" kind of evening.

- Fill an outdoor washing tub or bucket with ice and keep beverages cool indoors.
- Keep extra pillows and blankets on hand for comfy floor seating.

The Library

Meals shared surrounded by books naturally create an endless flow of chatter. And if the conversation lags, there are plenty of things to jump-start it sitting on the shelves.

- Steal a stack of books to create a centerpiece for your dining table.
- Clear a book shelf to use as a buffet or a self-serve cocktail bar.

Large Rooms

Essential when the guest list dictates space. I try to add lots of charm with vignettes, flowers, and fabulous centerpieces.

- Set up an extra table as a fantasy dessert bar.
- A wine and cheese bar in the center of a room brings guests and conversations together.

The Kitchen

Beginning the evening in the kitchen sets a tone for a "family"-style evening, where everyone pitches in and gets involved. It may be more chaotic, but a brilliant icebreaker for introducing someone new into a tight-knit group.

- Think of what you can learn from watching someone else's cooking.
- Use a garden ornament as a centerpiece to turn an ordinary kitchen counter into an extraordinary buffet.

Outside

I love to create rooms outdoors, and they can have such a different feeling depending on where you are and what you're doing. A simple setup of table and chairs makes a lovely tea in the garden—not much else is needed when the beauty of flowers surrounds you. For a picnic, make sure you choose a spot with a view. Then spread out on the lawn and drag out some of the comforts of home: comfy cushions, throws, and a wicker chest or a low, lightweight table. At night, create an outdoor tent near a tree. Hang candle lanterns for light; tie silverware to branches with string and let their chimes sing in the breeze.

The Table

Rectangular or long tables tend to break conversations off in many directions, while round and square tables lend themselves to keeping everyone chatting together. Of course, if your family is anything like mine, a minimum of four conversations are being held at any given time. Everyone in my family really likes to talk!

- For a change of pace, try dinner around the coffee table seated on big fluffy cushions.
- Table's too short? Add some space by putting smaller tables around or flanking your current table.

The Lighting

For a lunch or breakfast that can't be held outdoors, the room where sunlight streams through the windows is my ideal. Daylight adds such a warmth to any room, and it does wonders for the look of flowers, crystal, and glass. In the evening, I'm usually the first one to dim the lights and let my forehead relax. Candlelight is extremely magical, and the fireplace adds warmth to the chill of winter. The first thing I do when I walk in the door on a cold night is get my fireplace going. I love dimmer switches that let you control the lighting. Lamps and chandeliers are stunning in the evening with just a slight glow.

I try to infuse a little fantasy into my dinnerware designs, so at least the dishes make the table special when I need to pull it together in a hurry.

Getting set for a wonderful occasion is a labor of love for me. These darling little cherubs look as if they're preparing a fantasy celebration of their own.

$\mathcal{T}$hose of you who've seen my first book, *Dreams from Home,* may already know my belief that **"more is more."** The idea is that having a little bit of everything in life is the way to go. I guess this chapter on preparing for the rituals of entertaining redefines that concept. Once you determine what you need, you're on your way to making every day a little more special. No better time than the present to get started.

Listen, I'm not suggesting that you run out and stock up on all your entertaining paraphernalia today. I'm more of a gather-as-you-go kind of person—a pack rat of the extreme breed. So save stuff. I'm serious! I've developed a stash of oddball stuff that I liked just because something about it was quirky enough to *pique* my interest. And I'm constantly relying on that stash when I set a table or decorate a treat for a guest.

No matter where you are, keep your "collecting" radar ready. You can almost bet there's some kind of treasure waiting to be discovered. Allow yourself the luxury of time to dig around—finding cool stuff is part of the journey.

Part of being prepared for impromptu and planned events starts with pulling a ditzing kit together. First, you go on a fishing trip, for me this means gathering all the goods—scour, gather, scrounge, and discover elements that you can keep in your own bag of tricks. I'm a pack rat so I keep my stash on my goody cart until the need for organization becomes essential. When I'm feeling so inclined, I set time aside to organize my goods!

Keeping my goody cart well stocked is one of my favorite things, and I admit that I'm the tiniest bit obsessed. I'll drive for miles to our local craft store in search of artificial flowers for the mere pleasure of coating them with spray adhesive and sprinkling them with fairy dust (dime-store glitter). The obsession doesn't end when I'm traveling either—I'm always on the hunt. But who can blame me? Take a look at all the goodies on these pages—they are absolute deliciousness to me!

Goodie Cart

Whether you're making your own goody cart or you're just curious to know what's inside of one, we created this list as a reference. Don't break the bank—the idea is to use what you have; if you want to add to your supplies, refer to our grid (right).

Getting It to Stick

- spray adhesive
- hot-glue gun
- velcro
- glue sticks
- Elmer's glue
- a variety of pins
- needles and thread
- florist foam
- chicken wire
- tacks
- decoupage glue
- nails/hangers/screws/brads

Trimmings

- rickrack
- ribbons
- tassle fringes
- brush fringes
- yarn
- cording
- crinkle wire
- beaded or sequined trims

Fabrics: Types & Prints

- tulle
- velvet
- silk
- scraps/remnants
- dish towels
- vintage prints
- terry cloth
- linen
- ticking
- floral patterns
- solids
- prints

Tools

- scissors, a variety
- needle-nose pliers, wire cutters
- Envirotech resin
- artificial snow
- paint
- oil pastels, markers, crayons
- sealing wax
- screwdrivers
- hammer
- electric sander
- blowtorch (for you diehards)
- paintbrushes
- paper hole punch

Goodie Cart

Fluff

- feathers
- feather boas
- artificial flowers, fruits, and foliage
- buttons
- plastic toys
- charms
- seashells
- beaded flowers
- birds
- reindeer moss
- silk butterflies and insects
- playing cards
- empty containers

Sparklies

- rhinestones
- glitter
- sequins
- crystals
- silver and gold leaf
- glass beads
- marbles
- metallic thread
- metallic paint

Paper

- tracing, tissue, waxed paper
- parchment
- corregated paper
- wallpaper
- florist foil
- doilies
- wrapping paper
- plastic/paper tableware
- magazines, newspapers
- color copies
- cellophane
- labels, tags, stickers
- candy wrappers

Sugary Sweet Stuff

- cake decorating supplies
- candy necklaces
- fortune cookies
- suckers/lollipops
- foil-wrapped coins
- gumdrops, lemon drops
- candy sticks
- dragées
- frosted cookies
- nonpareils
- jelly beans
- holiday candy
- anything in a pretty wrapping

little pretties

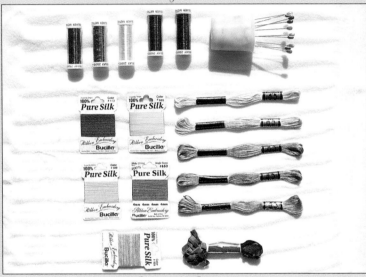

silken threads

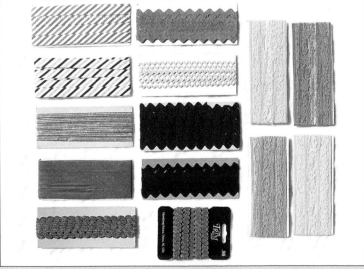

rickrack & trimmings

Cool Pack-Rat Destinations

Grocery Stores

- Think pastel instead of Snicker's the next time you are in search of candy for entertaining.
- Have you ever actually cruised the party goods aisle? The pseudo toy aisle?

Check out the bakery and ask if they will sell you any of those great decorations from their cakes.

Ethnic Grocery Stores

- Asian markets are my favorite. Great paper goods, pretty candies, fabulous packaging, wonderful newspapers, inexpensive chopsticks, bamboo mats, and more.
- Hispanic markets often have great candles, colorful piñatas, and fun candy.

Craft Stores

- Have you ever really looked at all of the great beads, baubles, feathers, and sparkles that exist? It's unbelievable.

Gumball Machines

- Where do they get that stuff?!

Dime Stores

- Hello! Great Stuff! Especially in toys, costume jewelry, and accessories, but take time to walk every aisle. Never know what you might find.

Party Stores, Dollar Stores

- Some of my most unexpected and inexpensive finds have shown up here.

Big Discount Department Stores

- Don't get me or anyone at our studio started on this subject. These stores are the coolest resources for housewares, party goods, kids, candy, and more.

Candles

Definitely part of every day for me. Even if I'm at home alone, I love the ritual of lighting candles and dimming the lights. It completely changes my state of mind, allows me to click off one part of my day and prepare for evening. Candles bring enchantment and warmth into any time of day. Since I burn them every day, I keep a good stock on hand and usually find the best bargains at discount stores and candle outlets.

Fairy Dust

Okay, I definitely get a little carried away with glitter. There are really no rules when it comes to this stuff—sprinkle it anywhere. For those who remember those fabulous school projects, glitter does take on a life of its own. You never know where it's going to end up, but you count on at least a speck of it making its way to the tip of your nose. We have a saying at the studio: *Go glittered or go home!*

One of my favorite ways to use it is to sprinkle it on the table before I set it. By the end of the meal, everyone is shimmering. At the farm, whether it's business or fun, it's rare that anyone escapes without a little hint of glitter.

Colors

Pastels, crayons, colored pencils, markers, and paints. You don't have to spend a fortune, but keeping some of this stuff on hand lets you add quick, colorful touches when you need to. Gold and silver metallic pens are magical!

A lot of these coloring tools can be used to transform an item that just feels "too new." A lot of these coloring tools can be used to give character, whether to an urn for flowers, or for transforming paper for an invitation from looking crisp and new to vintage and faded. Take a risk and alter at will!

A charming old-fashioned pantry stocks jars, cans, and bulk items for cooking. Our own Cabbage Rose wallpaper design on the doors makes this pantry great for display.

The Pantry

Peeking into someone's pantry is a bit like looking into his or her medicine cabinet. You might be surprised at what you find. The following is a list of things I tend to rotate in and out of the pantry, depending on my needs. It's meant to inspire—perhaps it will give you a new idea for a recipe.

Herbs and Spices (Fresh or Dried)

- rosemary, thyme, oregano
- tarragon, cilantro
- ginger
- shallots, garlic
- sea salt
- tellicherry peppercorns
- parsley, dill, mint
- allspice
- chili powder, paprika, anise
- cinnamon, cloves
- cardamom
- vanilla beans

Condiments

- balsamic vinegar
- rice vinegar
- tarragon vinegar
- olive oil
- walnut oil
- flavored mustards
- vegetable oil
- jams, preserves, chutney
- salsa, hot sauces
- safflower mayonnaise
- coffee, tea
- maple syrup, honey
- tapenade

Pickled and Marinated Yummies

- asparagus
- artichoke hearts
- hot Gardinierra
- capers
- jalapeños
- sun-dried tomatoes
- roasted red peppers
- olives—Kalamata, Sicilian, cured, dried, niçoise, Moroccan

Some Dried Basics

- macadamia and pine nuts
- slivered almonds
- sunflower seeds
- pasta: orzo and the zillion others
- rice: basmati, jasmine, wild, risotto, Arborio
- dried beans
- quinoa, millet, cracked wheat
- oatmeal
- lentils: green, red, yellow
- Carr's table water crackers
- tapioca, couscous

The Pantry

Dry Storage Fruits and Veggies

- apricots
- figs
- raisins
- dates
- mushrooms
- cherries

Canned Goods

- tomatoes
- baby corn
- peanut butter
- hot fudge
- mandarin oranges
- broths/stocks
- white northern beans
- black beans
- white asparagus
- grape leaves

Meat/Fish

- Rosette de Lyon salami
- Soppressata salami
- prosciutto
- canned oysters
- sardines
- anchovies
- canned salmon
- caviar

Goodies for the Fridge and Freeze

- butter
- cream cheese
- sour cream
- coffee ice cream
- vanilla ice cream
- Stilton
- white cheddar
- Parmigiano-Reggiano
- Asiago
- aged Gruyère
- Morbier

I love millinery goods, and they remind me of my Grandma Lucy whose closet overflowed with all of this wonderful stuff. But love them as I may, they can be expensive. We discovered that an inexpensive way to buy millinery flowers and fruits is to scour rummage sales for vintage ladies' pieces. The hat usually costs about the same price as a single vintage flower in an antique store, and often there are millinery goodies covering the entire hat.

Here's a thought. . . . Try your hand at creating easy and inexpensive sugared flowers—this process has changed the way I look at millinery flowers. I was at the craft store eyeing all the artificial flowers, which typically don't thrill me, when suddenly I imagined a way to make them fun—sugared flowers! Clip off their long stems, then add a little spray adhesive and a sprinkling of fairy dust (very fine glitter). They are transformed from fake to fantasy. Just imagine these flowers sitting in a circle of sparkling sugar on your table.

A fabulous table doesn't have to take a lot of time. Layers of different texture can bring it together easily. I try to think of the table as a landscape waiting to unfold. For inspiration I use unexpected combinations—silver and crystal, feathers and velvet, ceramic and wood. I think of all that pattern on pattern, add in some objects with scale and dimension, and before I know it I've created something that tickles my guests.

Do you dream in color?

For the Table

At right is a list of options to consider when planning your next table. Some you may already use; some may be things you have, but never move from the back of your cupboard (perhaps they'll get some use after you've read this book). Others may be things you've never considered but will put on next year's Christmas list. No need for any objects for the table to be boring, pack an open mind, consider a range of textures, colors, shapes, sizes. Variety is the spice of life!

- fork
- knife
- spoon
- tongs
- hors d'oeuvre knives, spoons, forks
- chopsticks
- pie server
- ladle
- salt spoons
- hors d'oeuvre picks

- platter
- charger
- tureen
- canapé dish
- cake stand
- tray
- bowl

- vase
- pitcher
- tins
- perfume bottle
- compote
- teacup
- canning jar
- urn

- martini
- wine
- champagne
- cordial
- double old-fashioned
- highball
- bistro
- áperitif glass
- sake cup

For the Table

- taper
- votive
- pillar
- tea light
- birthday

- dinner plate
- salad plate
- dessert plate
- saucer
- bowl

- napkin
- tablecloth
- place mat
- runner
- kitchen towel
- throws
- scarves
- fabric remnants

- salt and pepper shakers
- bird's nest
- basket
- candy
- crystal
- fortunes or quotes
- placecard holder
- napkin ring
- candleholder
- cloche

John and I happen to love our food and drink, so keeping a well-stocked pantry and bar can make an impromptu gathering a pleasure instead of a hassle. In the cocktail department, we try to stock a variety in our bar. John has been known to make a mean margarita and his version of a *drag-it-through-the-garden* Bloody Mary is notorious. My French roots have probably influenced my love of red wine, but I don't claim to know much about it other than what suits my own palate. Since I have a lot to learn I try to ask questions of anyone I meet who has knowledge of the subject. For me it's mostly about trial and error.

Having a summer gathering? Consider creating a serve yourself outdoor bar—perhaps an unusual old dresser or cabinet would be easy to transform!

The Bar

Whether you've got a party planned or not, it never hurts to be stocked. When unexpected company arrives, if you can't serve them a five-course meal you can always offer them something to drink. Use this list to keep the basics on hand.

Red Wine and Other Lovelies

- red wine
- white wine
- champagne
- port
- sherry
- cassis
- Cointreau
- Pernod

Tools

- corkscrew
- bottle opener
- cocktail shaker
- strainer
- tongs
- blender
- stir stick
- whisk
- sharp knife
- cutting board
- ice bucket
- cocktail skewer
- cocktail napkin
- straw
- coaster
- jigger

Light and Dark Beers

- ale
- porter
- stout
- red

Spirits

- triple sec
- vodka
- tequila
- rum
- vermouth
- Scotch
- gin

The Bar

Snackers

- tortilla chips and salsa
- peanuts in the shell
- pickled herring
- pretzels
- flavored popcorn
- olives
- cheese and crackers
- assorted salami

The Fixins

- lemons, limes
- olives
- pickled mushrooms
- maraschino cherries
- cream
- cocoa
- horseradish
- Worcestershire sauce
- Tabasco
- kosher salt
- sugar

Nonalcoholic Mixers

- Coke
- tonic water
- grenadine
- ginger ale
- bottled water
- lime aid
- fruit and vegetable juices

Into the Evening

- dessert wine
- Grand Marnier
- cognac
- Anise liquor
- Kahlúa
- Drambuie

Music takes any experience right over the top for me. I love the way an opera transforms my routine even if I'm just setting the table or washing dishes. This piece of artwork was created in our studio, inspired by the magic of nature's music. We call it BirdSong.

Classical Drama

- Patricia O'Callaghan, *Youkali*
- Cecilia Bartoli, *Chant D'Amour*
- Minantologia
- Andrés Segovia, *The Segovia Collection* (Volume I)
- Abby Newton, *Crossing to Scotland*
- Seong-Hyung Kon, *Dramatic Baritone Arias*
- Jussi Björling, *Operatic Arias* (1936–1941)

Torch and Romance

- Diana Krall, *Love Scenes*
- Andrea Marcovicci, *I'll Be Seeing You*
- Eartha Kitt, *Miss Kitt to You*
- Billie Holiday, *Billie's Blues*
- Karen Akers, *Presenting Karen Akers*
- Jeanie Bryson, *Some Cats Know*
- Sirens of Torch, *Classic Torch Singers*
- Nina Simone, *The Great Nina Simone*
- Peggy Lee, *Black Coffee & Other Delights*
- Dinah Washington, *For Those in Love*
- Cassandra Wilson, *Blue Light 'till Dawn*

Love It Anytime!

- Dan Fogelberg, *Greatest Hits*
- Mandy Patinkin, *Oscar & Steve*
- Bette Midler, *The Divine Miss M*
- Tom Jones, *The Complete Tom Jones*
- Van Morrison, *Moondance*
- James Taylor, *Greatest Hits*
- Bread, *Anthology of Bread*
- Jim Croce, Best of
- John Lee Hooker, Best of
- Dianne Warwick, *The Dionne Warwick Collection*

International Sounds

- Quinteto da Paraiba (Brazilian)
- Ensemble Romulo Larrea, "Le tango de chez nou"
- Edith Piaf, "*Non, je ne regrette rien*"
- Antonio Carlos Jobim, *A arte de Tom Jobim*
- Cesaria Evora, *Cabo Verde*
- Stan Getz and Joan Gilberto, Getz Gilberto
- Jesse Cook, *Gravity*
- Madredeus, *Ainda*
- Cesaria Evora, *Miss Perfumado*

Music

Movin' and Groovin'

- *Pure Disco 2*
- Lena Horne, *Ain't It the Truth*
- Al Green, *I'm Still in Love with You*
- Ella Fitzgerald, *Best of the Songbooks*
- The Fifth Dimension, *Greatest Hits on Earth*
- Marvin Gaye, *The Last Concert Tour*
- Barry White, *All-Time Greatest Hits*

Sound Tracks

- Eve's Bayou
- The Piano
- Betty Blue
- Big Night
- Diva
- The Sound of Music
- Lisbon Story
- Out of Africa

Holiday

- Vince Guaraldi, *A Charlie Brown Christmas*
- Anything by Bing Crosby
- Nat King Cole, *Chestnuts Roastin'*
- *A Celtic Christmas* (Love them all)
- Shirim, *Klezmer Nutcracker*
- Meryl Streep and George Winston, *The Velveteen Rabbit*
- Etta James, *12 Songs of Christmas*
- Ella Fitzgerald, *Wishes You a Swinging Christmas*

Girl Power

- Helen Reddy, *I Am Woman*
- Loreena McKennitt, *To Drive the Cold Winter Away*
- Carole King, *Natural Woman— Ode Collection*
- Joni Mitchell, *Clouds*
- Aretha Franklin, *Greatest Hits*
- Bessie Smith, *The Collection*
- Sweet Honey in the Rock, *Live at Carnegie Hall*
- Patsy Cline, *The Birth of a Star*

Silver~
all dressed up and no place to go but onto your
fabulous table. The handles of this silver get a taste of ribbons,
millinery leaves, flowers, and vintage jewelry. A dab of hot
glue will set them for any occasion.

CHAPTER 3

Dime-store Treasures and Other Fun Stuff

Adding the Fluff!

I could easily call this chapter "The Meaning of Life as I Know It." What could be better than all that little junk besides thinking of new ways to use it for your next event? If you were paying attention in chapter 2, you've had a prep course in all the little stuff that's so great to have on hand. Now that you've got it, you need to know what to do with it. And this, my friend, is where you really get to play! When I try to think about what makes a house enchanting or an occasion inspiring, for me it's in the attention to special details. In the studio we refer to this as "ditzing" or "adding the fluff."

What I love about using these little tchotchkes is the fact that they can take almost any occasion over the top without spending a ton of money. Reuse what you have in new ways. Add a layer of fluff and watch basic become bold or change the mundane to magnificent. It's all about giving your guests one special detail to appreciate or remember. It's the way we sprinkle a little magic into the mix.

First, look at all of the stuff you've got all around you and ask yourself, "What do I have that I really don't love? Maybe it's a platter? Or a tablecloth that needs a lift? Is there a way to change it to make it fabulous?" If your answer is yes, then you're on your way. We've tried to give some ideas on the following pages, but I'd encourage you to dream with your eyes open. If you don't see the exact solution to transform your particular junk, don't give up. Try to visualize how you might use our ideas for your stuff. If you're a dime-store treasure novice, get ready—it's time to take action! For those of you with an acquired-over-time collection, we hope you make some new discoveries on your journey through this chapter.

Start by making a list of your dime-store inventory and then play around with unusual combinations. Remember, it's the mix, not the match. So let those unlikely combinations be transformed into something wonderful.

A basic vanilla layer cake gets a makeover with candy, cookies, fabric trims, and a paper dragonfly. Bring a color chip to your baker, and ask him or her to match it for frosting.

To Tickle Your Fancy

Walter the Weimy discovers a chandelier while
treasure hunting with Mom.
Shown here pre-fluff—Imagine the possibilities . . .

Adding the fluff. Here's what you can do with feathers. Start with collecting them, from everywhere. Look outside, check old hats and vintage clothing. Craft stores sell feathers by the bag in every color and size, in a multitude of textures. Feather boas can be found at fabric stores, toy stores, and discount stores. Think exotic feathers, too—peacock and pheasant feathers are gorgeous!

- Serve tarts or petit fours with a few pink feathers on the plate and topped with dessert.
- Tuck one into the next invitation you send.
- Tie a feather boa around a basic silver pail and create an over-the-top champagne bucket.
- Dust them with fine glitter and lay one next to each place setting on your table.
- Stitch one feather simply into each corner of a napkin—it's sure to delight.

And the *va va va voom* after . . . a
beautifully embellished chandelier can easily become a centerpiece in your entertaining haven. The great thing about chandeliers
is that you can "dress them up" for different occasions. I love my
hanging beauties to reflect the spirit of a new season!

Paper indeed! These cups come in many colors at most party stores. The fun starts here, pull out your ditzing kit and go! Here we've added simple touches like ribbons, flowers, faux jewels, masking tape, plastic farm animals, stickers, and wax seals. And . . . Hello! What an awesome project to do with children!

At right we've created some whimsical ideas to inspire you to play around with embellishing your glasses at home! Cheers!

small Embellished
bird.

old Teacup....

6 fortune wound around handle

Butterfly

fanciful
ribbons

bubblegum
machine rings

Silky Threads.

Velvet Jackets....

buy A set
of cheap
glasses

leave
at least
1" open
at top

Strips of
velvet ribbons
glued on

A variety of Shapes and
Sizes on Your Table....

create a necklace with wire and
crystals

drop a
votive in
Your favorite
wine glass

a bed of flower
petals

base wrapped
in Tulle

Plastic Champagne flutes

leave
2" open
at Top for
lip Service....

from here down...
coat with Spray
adhesive .....then
dust with glitter

small millinery flowers.

Slipper For Your Wine Glass

glass slides
in through
this
opening

ric-rac
on Top

2 Pieces of fabric glued together

Perfume and Martinis

glue on
some pink
rhinestones

eau de.....

have Your girlfriends over for
cocktail — tie a sample of Your
favorite Scent on with a ribbon...

Find Very inexpensive glasses....

Keep 1" at
rim untouched
(health stuff)

fabulous Stickers — then Brush
on four coats of clear laquer or
acrylic polyurethane.

sugar the
rim

glue on
Some Vintage
flowers.

Vintage
necklaces

Pull out your goodies and make simple votives festive with ribbons, glitter, buttons, fake jewels, and beads.

Magic candy wands—the stuff dreams are made of! Make them dazzling by adding a sampling of treasures. Add a label and you've got a fanciful place card or a yummy idea for a gift tag. This photo inspires me to set my next table—I can imagine ballerinas twirling on a bed of feathers around each guest's goblet.

Chipped ceramics look sweet with the help of dime-store treasures! This little darling was saved from the trash, and now it makes a charming serving dish for cookies or dresses up a blank spot on a wall.

Make fantasy drink stirrers or straws. Imagine your grandmother sipping out of one of these at your next family gathering!

Adding some sparkle—

by now, you probably get the idea that creating the special effect of playing with dime-store treasures is about adding layers to ordinary and basic things. Adding a layer of sparkle can be enchanting, playful, and incredibly elegant. It's easy to get addicted. Try on these ideas:

Glitter

Have you ever really looked at glitter in the stores? The offerings will blow your mind! I love the very fine dust that comes in a range of pastel colors.

Depending on what you are putting it on, you may not need adhesive. Sometimes I like to sprinkle it on the dining table before I set it. Spray adhesive is great when you want the glitter to really stick to an object. Good to know: Once the adhesive dries, it loses its flammability.

- Glitter taper candles for your next dinner party.
- Lightly dust some on small birds, flocked animals, and paper butterflies. Shake off the excess and perch them anywhere.

- Use as the first of many layers on almost any object: the base of a chandelier, a candelabra, or an urn to be used for a centerpiece.
- Line the edges of place cards, table runners, coasters, and place mats.
- Sprinkle on inexpensive artificial flowers.
- Add glitter to a clear glass vase holding flowers; it'll get special notice with some sparkle in the water.

Other Good Sparklies

- Sequins (The assortment is a fantasy in itself!)
- Sew or glue some onto table linens
- Sprinkle them on your tabletop—gives an effect similar to glitter and easier to clean up!

Rhinestones

- Have an old platter? Add a few to its rim with glue.
- Add one to the handle of flatware.
- As a centerpiece, use a clear glass bowl filled with water, floating candles, fresh blooms, and some sparkle.

Marbles, Glass, Beads

- Scatter at the base of a centerpiece.
- Fill an old box with them and then add pillar candles.
- String beads to wind around the stem of a goblet.

Crystals

Can be found at lighting stores, craft shops, antique stores. Or do a search on the Internet. They are available in a variety of sizes, shapes, colors, and textures.

- Attach crystals to several branches with metallic silver and gold threads. Arrange in an oversize vase and place on your table.
- Tie a napkin around a crystal, and embellish with a favorite quote.
- Use metallic threads in silver and gold to attach crystals to several branches. Arrange in an oversize vase and place on your table.
- Make a necklace of crystals for huge pillar candles.
- Color with pastel markers, and they'll look like they're straight from Murano, Italy.

More ideas for dressing up plates and platters. Hot glue is easy to remove—it peels right off once it dries, so even my good dishes get a little glamour.

A variety of trinkets and treasures transform plastic flatware. What tiny bits and bobs do you have in your kit?

A garage sale candelabra. Before . . . and after. Table accoutrements arrive on the table in style. Just a bit of trim and some flowers added onto this piece take it to a whole new place! And the beauty of ditzing is that you can keep adding layers of embellishments or change it at a whim.

Feel free to experiment. . . .
There are no mistakes!

Fake Flowers, Berries, and Foliage

For vintage beauties, scour flea markets and antique stores for old hats and clothing. These are often made with real silks and velvets, each one is a prize. Mix the old with the new and use some of the ideas here to alter what you find. If an artificial piece looks too new and perfect, don't be afraid to dirty it up and give it a little character.

- Attach these gems to anything: platters, wineglass stems, candles, champagne bottles, flatware, and more.

- Use Envirotech, a resin product found in craft stores, to achieve a hard, glasslike finish on flowers. Or dip them in melted wax for a slightly softer finish.

- Pull fake flower heads from stems, dust with fine glitter, set on wax paper and coat with resin.

- To "age" flowers, try staining them with tea, rubbing them with oil pastels, or painting them with brown watercolors.

- For a soft and tattered look, try throwing foliage, flowers, and a pair of canvas tennis shoes in a laundry bag and running them through the dryer.

- Lay the piece on cement and use an electric sander to rough it up a bit.

- Add rhinestones for a little shine.

Aging things

At the studio, we use the expression "the imperfections of charm." This is our way of saying we love character flaws—they endear us to many of our possessions, and to people for that matter. For whatever reason when something is not so perfect, I am most drawn to it. The imperfection of its charm speaks to me. Funny as it sounds, when I can't find the flaws in a thing, I go out of my way to add them.

Here are some quick ideas to alter stuff that feels too brand spankin' new.

- Tea or coffee. Make a strong brew and use it to spray, dip, or brush on the piece depending on the look you want. Try this on ribbons, fabrics, photos, flowers, ceramics, and more.

- Burning. *Be extremely careful!* We keep a small propane torch in the studio and it really docs the trick on edges of paper, wood, fabrics, and more. Make sure you wear goggles and leather gloves, and use your torch outside only.

- Dirt. That's right—just drag your things in it. Rub it on, stomp it on, or pretend you're seven years old again and try washing it in a dirt bath.

- Bottled inks, dyes, and watercolors. These work great when watered down—dip and dunk. For a marbled, mottled effect, twist and tie with string, tie-dye style!

- Fake snow spray. I always stock up at Christmastime. Use it to transform fake foliage and flowers. Great combined with spray paint and glitter!

- Water. For anyone who's had a leaky roof, you know what kind of damage it can do. In this case, your next rain shower may add the perfect finish to your "too perfect" things.

- Bleach. Great for fading and breaking down fibers.

- Cola. This stuff is powerful! If used for a long enough time, it can eat through nails.

- Mineral oil. Adds a greasy finish. Combined with oil pastels, the effect can be beautiful on wallpaper and wood.

- Sandpaper. Alters a finish. Use a power sander when you need more strength to get the job done.

- Salt or sand. Combine with paint to add texture to wood, paper, ceramics, and other materials.

- Hammer. Use to create a few flaws, if necessary!

Note: Whatever you try, use extreme caution! Always wear eye protection, work outside when dealing with fire, and don't mix chemicals or household cleaners; the combination can cause toxic fumes.

Is it possible for paper plates actually to be this delicious? We added Hawaiian fake flower leis, dainty trims, and pretty stickers to these.

With each of the ten layers we added to her, this angel gets more personality. She was so plastic and perfect when we bought her. Then, with old wallpaper, a little dirtying up, some flowers and oil pastels, she could almost pass for an heirloom centerpiece handmade by a dear old aunt. When you're out antiquing, try to notice all the lovely details in vintage pieces.

Party girl Deb hangs her invites on the line!
Have some fun, it's all about permission to play!

CHAPTER 4

Guess Who's Coming to Dinner?
Invitations with a Twist

Since I was a kid, I've always loved making things. I'm sure that's why I get so excited about all of the special touches that go along with having people over. Immediately, I start thinking, "How should I entice everyone to come? How will I make this experience different from the last?" I have a tight group of friends and since many of us work, travel, and play together, it gets a little challenging to surprise my guests because my list is fairly constant.

I like to set the tone for the evening with the invitation. I imagine my friends at the mailbox opening something that looks as if my peacock, Zelda, must have delivered it. The more outrageous the better. A little foreshadowing is always fun with invitations—think of them as a taste of what's to come.

An invitation created by hand can be a keepsake that holds the vision of an event alive and vivid in our memories. Why not use the invitation in an album or scrapbook that contains photographs of the celebration?

A store-bought invitation embellished by hand can be just as special as something made from scratch. In my book, this means it's okay to cheat a little bit. Hey, we're all busy, and we reserve the right to cut corners to save time when we need it. Using a time-saver doesn't mean you have to compromise on specialness. Occasionally, I find a store-bought invitation that I love, and I'll decorate it a little to add a twist.

My goody cart always comes in handy for invitations. I mean, once you've got all that great stuff to work with the combinations are endless. Think of a hand-painted invitation layered with stickers, buttons, and beads. Or antique photographs fancied up with rickrack and printed papers cut with pinked edges. Invitations don't have to be identical—in fact, this is a great way to use some of those one-of-a-kind treasures that you, the pack rat extraordinaire, have collected.

On the following pages you'll see some of the invitations that have been created, inspired, received, and sent by me and the cast of characters here at Stonehouse Farm. Many of these invitations remind me of cherished, hilarious, touching moments shared with friends and family. Whatever you create, enjoy the process and play a little.

A few clues, a little intrigue. How can you entice your guests? Perhaps with a marked map and clues that lead to the specific time, date, and occasion for the party.

Hints of what's to come—found objects, discarded trinkets and treasures, along with a handmade map. Is your next event a treasure hunt? A garden party? A baby shower? Think of elements inspired by those occasions.

A Chinese Tea Party

The simple idea that other cultures can inspire an afternoon. During our travels, we've found that Chinatown and ethnic grocery stores are great places to stock up on paper fans, Asian newspapers, chopsticks, and gift wrap. Silk threads and silver leaf add a finishing touch. Think of how a culture can inspire not only the invitation, but also every entertaining element from the favors to the food to the music. Even one element from another culture can put a fun twist on your party.

Here's an example of an invitation that we made. We found a paper fan at the Asian market for ten cents, cut an oval out of colored paper using decorative edged scissors, and used silk threads and a large sequin to attach our message.

A Handful of Posies

Make a special handmade gift that you deliver to your friend's door. This little beauty wears an invitation tag for lunch and makes a pretty vase of posies for the receiver. And, of course, when the weather permits, you can pick flowers from your own garden. A home-grown, hand-touched gift is a special way to let friends know you are extending an invitation to them.

Other handmade invitations might depend on your talents—a poem, a song, a tiny painting, a drawing, a handmade box, or a hand-sewn sachet.

37

Your Heart's Desire

What could be better for Valentine's Day than a romantic getaway? Wax seals, metallic papers, stickers, and labels make this invite an affair of the heart. Our valentine was cut with pinking sheers from pastel craft foam. A ribbon and pipe cleaners were woven into two punched holes (a great way to hang it). Layered with stickers and labels, wrapped in a swatch of tulle, and tucked inside a foil-covered envelope. A wax seal tops it off.

Other unusual materials to use:

- candy wrappers
- costume jewelry
- candy hearts
- wine bottle labels
- a pretty vintage handkerchief

Hollywood Nights

We have a tradition at the farm— on *Oscar night* we glitter up and enjoy champagne and hors d'oeuvres in front of the best available tube. Decked out in full Acadamy costume, we have ourselves a ball. If you haven't indulged, make this your year! My invitation is a collage of silver doilies, magazine cutouts, and printed paper. How can you go wrong? The television might be a great escape, but it has a way of cuing us to major events. For those who like an excuse to play, how about the Kentucky Derby, the Super Bowl, the Miss America Pageant, the Grammy Awards? Whatever floats your boat.

Surprise Party

When I was a kid, I thought those people at Cracker Jack really had the right idea with that treat in the box. Playing on their cue, what better invitation for a birthday party than one that comes in a Cracker Jack box! Invitations don't need to come in just envelopes.

Other ideas for unusual invitations:

- tucked inside a book
- wrapped around a candle
- baked into a fortune cookie
- marked on a beautiful calendar

I have a friend who once received a romantic invitation in a gallon of ice cream. Whoever left it there knew he wouldn't miss an evening with out dipping into his favorite dessert.

An engagement party certainly calls for a ring. First, raid your local gum ball machine. Then, cut craft paper with scissors and finish with stickers, watercolors, rickrack, and glue. Let whatever pops out of the gum ball machine decide the theme for your next party.

At our anniversary breakfast, I thought it would be romantic to make John an invitation. I created a special one in a box inspired by the original handmade box I gave him as a wedding gift. I love recycling an old idea in a new way. Just knowing John would be reminded of our special day provided me with all the inspiration I needed to make our celebration magical. Think of a gift that you've given your loved one that might trigger his or her memory of a special day, and find a way to use it to beckon him or her somewhere. It's one way to put all those special boxes, containers, and pretty packaging to use.

39

Each invitation can become a little adventure— explore with materials. Surely, this will get your creative juices flowing.

A poem or riddle that unveils details of an event can be created on a computer, contrasting the tactile and hand-touched details of this invite. Paper board, tissue paper, stickers, and ribbons go over the top with rhinestones and feathers.

To celebrate new life we honor those we love with a baby shower. Bring bits of nostalgia and childhood memory into this invitation with candy, paper dolls, vintage coloring books, or pages from your favorite children's books. Decoupage and add goodies to the collage. The envelope can be just as pretty as what's inside!

GUESS WHO'S BACK IN TOWN!!!

A WELCOME HOME PARTY FOR
OUR LONG-LOST DEAR HEART

FRIDAY, NOVEMBER 28th - 6:00PM
LULU'S ON THE SQUARE

At the farm, we've declared ourselves "art nerds," but the one thing that we have in common is that there isn't a guru or expert in the bunch. I guess my friends and I are more like most of the people we know—we just want to add a special touch to anything we do, and we don't want to take too much time.

If you have the tools and know how to use them, then it's time to take the plunge. Even my friend Christine, who claims to not know how to sew on a button, discovered that she can operate a hot-glue gun. I really don't need to tell you how to do it—think layers, think more is more, and you're on your way!

A home rehab or construction project can be very stressful for the family. Let friends see the rubble so they can appreciate the finished work of art. Perhaps a bit of the antique wallpaper being scraped from the house could be the basis for an invitation. At any rate, putting down the tools long enough to gather friends and take note of your progress can be rejuvenating.

This anniversary breakfast setup is sure to delight friends and family for other occasions too.

CHAPTER 5

Charmed Mornings

My parents found this perfectly rusted iron table at a local estate sale.

Great flea market and auction finds often make their way to our store. That would be me, borrowing the table for my "outdoor room." You can be sure once I borrowed it, I'd never let it go.

I like to use what I already have. I've been known to dig into my pantry, closets, cupboards, and drawers to pull a table together. For me, it's all about mixing the old with the new.

How can I make our anniversary memorable? With champagne, tea biscuits, and sugared grapes *(least we forget our sweets)!* A lovely spring forecast means breakfast alfresco. John and I love the views on the property, so I decide on a peaceful spot in the garden where the ducks and geese are still in view.

Menu and location done, it's time to think of making the setting special. Standing in the garden is a lovely statue given to me by my parents, so I let her provide the inspiration for an "outdoor room." My thoughts turn to how I can use what I already have. I envision my own rugs and pillows, framed art, mirrors, and a rusted iron table and chair set from Mom and Dad's stash, all setting the stage for our day. A quick stop at a garage sale or the flea market might bring a discovery that adds the last special touch to our charmed morning.

My mind gets going with a list of ideas: a chandelier hanging in the trees, curtains hanging from a branch, perhaps a centerpiece that incorporates some of John's family photos. It doesn't really matter how many of these ideas I actually use—just getting them down on paper gives me a place to start.

We'll be surrounded by flowers in the garden, but we can still add fresh-cut arrangements to our setting. I make a note to pick a spot bursting with color. I keep a running checklist until I've found at least one idea to stimulate each of the senses.

- Touch—This table sings with a symphony of texture.
- Smell—The scent of flowers and candles fills the air.
- Sound—I love to listen to the "chitter-chatter" of the chickens and geese.
- Sight—We enjoy views of the garden.
- Taste—A country breakfast, sugared grapes, and champagne—need I say more?

Okay, so I did splurge a little on the champagne, but this is a morning to celebrate! Here's where I tried to cut some corners. Instead of a candelabra, I wound fresh-cut vines around tapers. The tablecloth was a vintage skirt collecting dust in my closet, and the silverware is all about mixing patterns and textures. The finishing touch? Mr. and Mrs. Matrimony standing on the centerpiece—by gently aging them, I made them look vintage. I like the antique sets from the 1930s but they're not easy to find.

Sometimes you have the most fun with one special touch that comes from using something basic. Pick something that's such a part of your everyday life you hardly even notice it, and discover its romance. I chose sugar as the basic-turned-fantasy for this occasion. Sugar is one of the great loves of my life. I'm convinced it has something to do with being deprived of a candy jar growing up in my parents' home!

When you think of a spoonful of sugar, consider the many ways to use it. Sugar is very pretty stuff—for all of its sparkle and shine, it deserves more than being dumped into morning coffee. Think sprinkle, dip, roll, and coat.

An old cigar box was transformed into a treasured keepsake holder for our wedding memories. This handmade box reminds me of the original that I gave John on our wedding day. Today, the replica holds a message inviting John to join me in the garden for a festive breakfast.

1

Vintage "pretty in pink" pillowcases were used for napkins, and wedding bells strung on a bit of netting (tulle) remind us of our special day.

Other little ditties for napkins:

- Sew rickrack along their edges.
- Cut edges into a scallop design.
- Sew charms to each corner with silver thread.
- Tie a tiny holiday ornament with ribbon and use as a napkin ring.
- Attach sugared flowers (see p. 17) to an elastic ponytail holder for a springtime ring.

2

Champagne anyone? Make mine baby blue (a drop of food coloring will do), sugar-coated, and wrapped with adorable candy necklaces.

Other things to serve in an elegant glass:

- fruit salad
- ice cream
- candy
- lemonade

3

When John and I abandoned Chicago, we didn't leave much behind but all those keys that city life demands. Since our urban-dwelling days, John has been the faithful keeper of the Stonehouse Farm keys. On our anniversary, I gave him some fanciful handmade key chains.

Other tiny handmade gifts:

- a lovely sachet filled with mint, rosemary, and lavendar
- a cutting of ivy or bulbs from the garden
- a pretty paper cone filled with sugar cubes and packets of tea

4

You know what they say about small packages. The gift box was sprayed with adhesive, rolled in rice, tied with ribbon and costume jewels, then finished with a love poem fastened with a pretty pin.

Other thoughts on wrapping:

- Use a box with a lid. Wrap the box in pretty paper and hot-glue a nest of flowers, birds, and berries to the center of the lid.
- Wrap a package in colored tissue paper, cut a strip of wallpaper with pinking shears and wrap around box as a decorative band. Use a pretty sticker label as the gift tag.
- Instead of using a bow, wrap a small gift with a feather boa or a length of tulle.

Every day life inspires creativity in our studio. This original painting is a collage of ideas and memories that evoke thoughts of romance.

Think Outside of the Box

Just because many of these ideas were inspired by our anniversary doesn't mean that they wouldn't be just as much fun to celebrate other occasions.

Hopeless romantics	Valentine's Day (If you live up north, take your celebration indoors.)
Gardeners	Any old spectacular summer morning.
Girlfriends	A great excuse to get together.
Siblings	When is the last time you shared a glass of champagne?
In-laws visiting for the weekend	They'll get a kick out of a candy necklace.
Birthday celebrants	Who says you can't celebrate in the morning?

Les Bonnes Idées

The Table

Plastic bride and groom	Sprayed with fake snow, rubbed with pastels, and sanded to age them
Tarnished silver compote	Antique stores, flea markets, tag sales
Flowers	Phlox fresh from the garden or florist
Goblets	Mine were wedding gifts, use what you've got. In a pinch they now come in plastic—don't forget to sugar the rims.
Candy necklaces	Great to wind on stems, napkins, candles, and ponytails!
Sweetarts	Sprinkle on the table.
Champagne	Add a touch of food coloring.
Sugared grapes	Any berry or sliced fruit works; try colored sugar
Teacups and dessert plates	It's the mix, not the match.
Feather fans	An interesting texture that adds a touch of whimsy to our table
Silk scarves	What else have you got in that closet?
Chair cushions	These are pillows from our very own home collection.
Chairs	Can always be dressed with ribbon, trims, paint, and flowers
Wedding bells	Plastic—we charmed ours up with pastels and sprayed with clearcoat acrylic.
Vintage pillowcases	Disguised as napkins

The Gift

Round paper boxes	Covered in spray adhesive and rolled in white rice
Hat pins, jewels	Auctions, estate sales, flea markets
Tags	This is where those pretty candy wrappers, labels, stickers, and paper come in handy. A handwritten message works like a charm.

The Invitation

Cigar boxes	Ask a cigar lover to save them for you.
Photos	Pick your favorite and one that suits your occasion.
Wallpaper	Old or new—think layering or use other scraps of paper for collage.
Feathers, tissue, tulle, rickrack	Craft store heaven
Millinery flowers	Vintage or glittered artificial flowers

The Food

Here are some quick options:

- Champagne, sugared grapes, and strawberry French toast
- Mint tea and lemon cookies
- Café au lait and warm, cinnamon-apple pie
- Chai tea and asparagus/prosciutto omelette
- Peach cobbler and luscious cream
- Angel food cake with a dollop of lemon curd

Enjoy the journey. A joyous
occasion spent with one that you
love is about feeding your soul.
In your efforts to pull it all
together, remember to relax and
find tranquillity in the experience.

An outdoor stone birdbath is filled with my best girly-girl goodies and then topped with glass to make an elegant table.

CHAPTER 6

Breaking the Table Setting Rules

kay, even though I like to break the rules, I appreciate the proper way to set a table. When we start our family, I know I'll want my children to understand those rules as much as I'll want them to behave politely and use their manners. I'd also like them to know they have the freedom to change the rules for themselves. I mean, having the knife to the left of the plate will not limit the dinner conversation. Nor will it change the taste of the pork chops. If the table feels fabulous and fun, then it's workin' for me.

The table can mean more than a set of pretty dishes; consider where you'll dine, the color, pattern, mixture of textures, and light. Play up each of these elements, and you're on your way to fantasy. Let yourself experiment, and take it one step at a time.

- **If you normally eat dinner in bright light, try dimming it or using candles. See how it changes the experience.**

- If you eat with the television on, try listening to classical music instead.

- **Before you overwhelm yourself hosting a party for ten, start with entertaining another couple. It's like anything else— you might need a little practice.**

- **If you have a large party planned and the idea of setting the entire table is daunting, try creating one place setting at a time.**

- **Afraid you don't have enough stuff to go around the table? Make each place setting different.**

- **Make a list—we did. Include stuff you know you have and would like to use.**

See the personality in what you own. Are you drawn to a particular look? Is everything sweet? Austere? Formal? Simple? Traditional? Do you want to keep going in that direction, or are you ready for something else?

If your dishes are sweet, does anything edgy appeal to you? Does something stop you from going there? Expand your table wardrobe—try on something new!

The best part of setting the table is in the playing; let something different inspire you every time you go into your cupboards. If your gathering already has a theme, well then, work it! If your gathering doesn't have a personality, give it one!

- *Alice-in-Wonderland tea*
- *a masquerade ball*
- *Hollywood in the 1930s*

You are not alone—enlist the help of others! The girls and I dug around in one another's closets, pantries, and cupboards to come up with what we hope will be food for thought the next time you create a distinctive table. Perhaps the elements we used will remind you of something you have. And why not borrow things from friends? At Stonehouse Farm, we trade all the time.

Ask yourself questions! We often get to the heart of the matter that way. Questions are the quickest way I know to jump-start the brain.

Can you find new and interesting ways to use what you already have?

- **an espresso cup filled with sugar cubes**
- **a candle vase filled with ice and set in a bowl— a great place to chill the champagne**

Ways to delight at the place setting of each guest? A votive and matchbook, a tiny flower, a simple quote, a before-dinner toast.

Setting the table is one of the great rituals of gatherings, but why not treat yourself to a fun place setting the next time you're dining alone? I believe the few moments of extra effort will be worth it as you take a moment to gather your thoughts over a delicious meal. Break the rules, and indulge yourself.

Framed butterfly art is used as a "place mat" for our
Orchard dinner plate. A peacock feather and delicate bird's nest complement a
richly colored bracelet used as a napkin ring. The flatware, salad plate, and olive green goblet
are an example of mixing new and old treasures.

Options:

• Look on your walls for artful inspiration for a table setting; this setting was inspired by a friend.

• Bring other rustic elements onto your table. Think of pine cones, leaves, acorns,
branches, and all the wonderful ways to wind them in.

Who says a glass should be restricted to hold a beverage. A playful Popsicle dessert course is served in elegant crystal.

C'mon, get out of the comfort zone.
- Shake it up! Eat just about anything with chopsticks.
- Give those salt and pepper shakers a rest and use the unexpected. Glue tiny paper flowers to shells and set at the place of each guest as a treat.
- Tiles make great utensil rests.

As much fun for adults as it is for children: This little ceramic dog warmed up my soup bowl on a rainy afternoon.

Go for color! If I want to make a statement with color on the table, I try to mix it up with a variety of patterns and textures.

Who wouldn't love to find a little rubber duck floating in their Fruit Loops? An enameled tin bowl sitting on china? Why not?

Flatware—I keep my eyes peeled for the silver wherever I go: I'm drawn to a variety of styles, and complete sets aren't necessary. Try this at home: salvaged architectural pieces make an interesting place for flatware and add some interest to the table.

Tickle a child's fancy with a *Forever Play* table.

CAT

I'm always delighted to imagine a child's view of the world; their approach to nearly everything comes from a fantasy place. Whatever they touch or talk about relates to playing—what will make it fun? So when I'm designing, decorating, or setting a table, I try to keep my mind open and dreamy, just as a child would.

Child's Play

- Toys—plastic cheapies are great
- Stickers—great on tablecloths
- Blocks
- Hand-painted glass—what child wouldn't love to make one?
- Ice-cream cones—great for holding candy, or Jell-o pudding
- Candy necklaces—kids love these
- Feather boas and hats—perhaps tonight they can "dress up" for dinner
- Comic books—Is there really anything wrong with reading at the table on special occasions?
- Kiddie cocktails
- Straws
- Plastic utensils—great for decorating
- Name tags—kids love to write their own name
- Craft paper tablecloth—with crayons at each child's place

FROG

DOG

Today's
Special

Moving through Blue.
Have you ever stopped to consider how
many shades of a color truly exist? We let the aqua
color of this room influence our selection of many blues
for this table for one. The velvet scarf from my closet
starts its next life as a table runner. The votives sparkle
with a dusting of glitter. Who says cooking and
eating alone can't be made fun?

I like my desserts and can't think of any more charming than petit fours. All that pastel-colored frosting, so delicious and pretty to look at. Here's a great example of my life's loves influencing my design—this new dinnerware sings of those darling tiny cakes in the softest hues. A desk painted in butter-cream colors makes a delightful base for this sweet scene.

When you first think of white, it's not very exotic. It's simple and basic, but it can be very interesting. Most people associate me with bursting color and layers of pattern, but I do get a charge out of white—like a fresh stack of clean, white towels. White is a clean resting place, but it can be ornate with pretty details or rough with texture. See white in a new way. Think in layers. Our first was soft, billowy white gauze on the table. Anything sheer adds a bit of intrigue; it's almost ethereal. The next layer is about texture—a rattan woven fan is neutral, but its pattern complements all the white without competing for attention. The third layer is mixing the look of dishes—a simple but elegantly embossed Wedgwood plate plays on milk glass with complicated cut patterns. Even sugar cubes served on an accoutrement plate add another white surface—utilitarian in texture but with a touch of sparkle. A one-of-a-kind architectural piece can be used as a spoon rest; if you need more ideas, try birch bark, a piece of coral, or a simple stone.

Serene rituals meet the exotic! I love tasting foods from many cultures. Japanese, Thai, African, Chinese, and Indian cuisines combine the most incredible spices to create delicious flavors. Let your favorite cultures influence how you dress your table tonight. The idea is that a combination of varied elements enhances the exotic feeling, even if each makes a different statement on its own.

A tattered Italian tapestry is used as a runner—remember it's okay that it's slightly worn; that adds character. The look of lamps on the table is created simply by adding shades to candles. We used a vintage linen dish towel as the napkin of choice, and we filled an elegant bowl with water and floating candles. What a treat for each of your guests! Even the autumn-colored paper doily and our colorful Myrtle Ivy dinnerware look slightly avant-garde in this setting. A variety of details in the glasses—hand-painting, embossed patterns, and silver. Perhaps one is for wine, one for water, and one for the chocolate mousse for dessert! Change your perspective—instead of eating at the dining table, throw some oversize cushions on the floor and eat at the coffee table with friends tonight.

Shake up your next holiday table.

Forget the predictable and let new colors, textures, and flowers from a different season set the tone. Our Viola Mint dinnerware looks fresh as spring for a winter holiday celebration. Antique postcards were used as place cards; to create an elegant table runner, some tassel trim was hot-glued to vintage flocked wallpaper.

Look for the things that make your eyes dance!

My cast of characters begins with my menagerie of animals at Stonehouse Farm. Find ways to bring your favorite animals into your next alfresco occasion. I cherish flocked birds, plastic farm animals, and ceramic statues. Look for colors or patterns in your dishes that will be complemented by another pattern on your table. The color of the leopard spots pulls my eye to the blacks and creams of our Sweet Briar Rose pattern, even though the main color of this plate is celadon cream.

Let a little nostalgia touch your table.

Vintage dinnerware from hotels, diners, vacation spots, and bars can add some kitschy kick to your grandmother's formal china. Remember, there is no need to take your place settings too seriously.

Photo at Left

Getting out of the comfort zone is what this scene is all about! Taking the most obscure objects you can find and combining them to create an unlikely, but positively outrageous result. We're serving something simple like alphabet soup on an elegant antique compote. The higher the soup bowl the closer to your lips, right? A tiny silver box holds decorative mixed beans and some tiny votives for each guest. Talk about lighting your fire—we couldn't resist a remnant of faux fur as a tablecloth. Chipped and tarnished plates are embellished with ribbons and cameos to disguise their flaws. Why not serve a lime Popsicle on crystal? Don't forget to garnish with your favorite hot pink bloom—we chose cosmos from my garden.

Photo at Right

Juxtaposition is all about changing your perspective. Look at stuff in a new light. Turn basic into unusual. Salt and pepper shakers are more intriguing when served in an antique lock. I love the idea that something once discarded can be infused with new purpose.

Photo at Left

Are you someone who thinks entertaining with paper and plastic is tacky? Get ready for a touch of fantasy. A plastic charger dish imitating crystal is layered with millinery flowers, glittered leaves, and paper butterflies, and then topped with an acrylic plate. Two petal-pink paper napkins are tied with string, cut with scalloped edges, and fluffed. The butterfly looks like it just landed on a rose. Straws, utensils, and stirrers get some whimsy with beads and baubles. An antique print makes a fine coaster.

Disposable or not, who would want to throw this stuff away?

Photo at Right

Get out of the closet. That's right; investigate what's lurking behind those doors, in the jewelry box, and stuffed in your drawers. I bet you've got more in there than you think! Here, my leopard scarf sings a different tune as a table runner, and some of my favorite jewels can dress up a friend's napkin for one night.

Lighting can make all the difference. I love the way sun bursts into our bedroom at daybreak, and how a fire's evening glow changes my mood. You can alter the whole experience of a room just by filling it with light in a new way.

Candles can create magic, but this antique lamp adds mysterious intrigue on it's own.

CHAPTER 7

Go Somewhere and Explore

I often refer to myself as an explorer—perhaps this is because I see my life as a journey. Whether I'm entertaining or in the studio, each day leads to an adventure, an experience that is completely new. Unexpected challenges do arise every single day—that much about life I've learned to be true. But the other lesson I've learned is that as long as you continue to push yourself out into the unknown, take a chance and be willing to try, you'll eventually realize that you're really more capable than you give yourself credit for.

This idea of living one's life as a journey was the inspiration for this chapter. Take this same idea of experiencing something you've never done before and apply it to the idea of entertaining. That's right, go somewhere and explore. If you live in the country, can you get out into nature? If you live in a city, can you get to a rooftop for a picnic? How about tea in a friend's garden shed? If you live near a lake, can you have a candlelit dinner on a dock? Can you take your grandmother on a bike ride and share a thermos of tea and scones?

Think of the special places and moments in time that conjure up memories for you. Think of places you've always wanted to travel and explore. Don't those daydreams stimulate your imagination? That's what happens to me when I enter a new kind of environment. My imagination kicks into gear: What would it be like to entertain here? Or, what would I do with this space?

My friends Maura and Deb own a wonderful store called Henry's just a few doors down from our own store in the town of Princeton. Its attic was loaded with boxes overflowing with memorabilia and rooms full of antiques. Every time I entered that building I got such a sense of what Princeton must have been like when the river trade was booming. I get a little lost on the second floor of Henry's. The staircase draws me up into a corridor with room after tiny, mysterious room. The space feels somewhat abandoned and has the musty aroma of a cottage that's been shut up all season. With its creaky pine floors, crumbling plaster walls, and peeling vintage wallpaper, you can easily imagine its life in years past. Deb and Maura have let me play in their home and garden shed for our various photography projects over the years, and this time they gave me carte blanche to explore and transform Henry's attic for a fantasy evening.

We begin the setup by unpacking dust-covered boxes looking for table setting treasures: a retro-looking kitchen set, a crazy quilt (our tablecloth), and tortoiseshell glasses sitting on vintage teacup saucers.

An old shaving mirror makes an unusual centerpiece topped with a floral hat. The best part of this table is that it's completely spontaneous. It feels a little quirky when it's finished, kind of like Mr. and Mrs. Howell discover the Secret of the Hidden Staircase. Basements, garages, and cellars are usually the best spots to redisover discarded treasures. Have you checked yours lately?

The intrigue of Henry's attic became the inspiration for the invitation.
A map and tale with clues lead our guests to the scene of an enchanted evening.

In the Attic

*I*t's all about improvising. We found a box of antique ashtrays that we used as salad plates. This kitschy set of diner coasters was given to Deb by her grandmother.

Don't forget to bring hand-me-downs into the experience—a bit of nostalgia sparks the memory.

I like using books on a tabletop. They give to the table dimension, height, and additional texture; they're especially lovely when opened to a pretty page.

Try to look at old junk from a fresh perspective. If you can't see your own stuff as more than junk, try swapping a couple of boxes with a friend. Beauty is definitely in the eye of the beholder.

While rummaging through boxes, we find stacks of old photographs and decide to create a wall of fame in honor of Princeton's former ancestors. A coat stand is strung with votives for a bit of ambiance, and Our Lady Mannequin becomes our impromptu guest of honor.

- Perhaps a coat stand becomes the spot where guests drop their coats and pick up a token gift or written message from the host.

- Think about scale—perhaps a coat stand perched on a table has a treelike presence. String it with votives and place tiny presents around the base.

String votives with nonflammable heavy-gauge wire and test them first. Use them safely, of course, and think of the possibilities! Tea lights gathered together in one big bunch could create the illusion of an unusual chandelier. I buy these in bulk at candle outlets, and often find a hundred tea lights for under ten dollars.

Now that invitations have been sent, the table is set, candles are lit, and walls are decked out, we're ready to plan the details. Since our evening is all about nostalgia, we decide to make up some old-fashioned favorites with a twist. Here's what we came up with:

Menu

- Serve pork chops with cilantro garlic pesto.
- Try mashed potatoes with a river of butter, sitting on a bed of crab or lobster .
- Our grandmothers deep fried everything. How about a spin on the traditional? Batter and deep-fry marinated artichoke hearts or roasted red peppers.
- How about a home-baked pie with a spirit for today? Apple-ginger? Strawberry-mint? Banana-lime-coconut cake? Think of making basic banana bread with a few extra touches.

The idea is to take an element from the setting, whether it's an old diner or your grandmother's table in 1934. I wish I had a diary of meals that my ancestors ate on special occasions—perhaps you could use this idea to pass on to your kids or grandchildren.

Music

- Pick a year, any year. Why not let a particular era inspire the music selection?
- Intrigue, mystery, and nostalgia. Prerecord a few old-time radio mystery stories and share them with your guests. (Ours air late on Sunday nights on Wisconsin Public Radio.)
- Tommy Dorsey has a way of taking me back in time. I love the scratchy, imperfect recordings of his 1940s swing. (Frank Sinatra cut more than eighty-three songs with the Tommy Dorsey Orchestra from 1940–1942.)
- Big-band sounds of the late 1930s, from Benny Goodman and the Glenn Miller Band.
- Edith Piaf adds a certain "je ne sais quoi" to an evening and makes me want another glass of wine!

Odds and Ends

- A tag sale table is easily transformed with a layer of wallpaper on top.
- Wallpaper also makes a nice wrapping for a bottle of wine. Add a touch of velvet ribbon and a delicious quote as an extra-special finishing touch.
- Use your own family photos to create a collage under glass on a table. Talk about a conversation piece—try this as a way to coax your relatives into sharing some of those secret family stories!
- I am intrigued with the concept of "under glass." Imagine a row of glass garden cloches set on top of decorative cake plates for serving dessert? What other ways can you creatively bring glass onto your table?

We take a moment to reflect on the many lives that touched this small town far before we ever knew it existed. Tonight we make a toast to Princeton, Wisconsin—the cast of characters that came before us and those who will come long after we are gone.

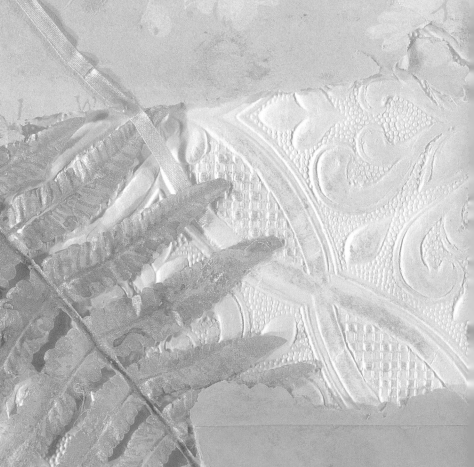

Explore. You never know what you might find.

How can I resist robbing the garden of its many charms? A contemplative cement garden ornament given to us by John's mom, loosely wrapped in recycled chicken wire, makes a great place to add a touch of my beaded flower collection.

CHAPTER 8

The Quintessential Centerpiece
Making It All Work Together

Conceptualizing a centerpiece is a bit like theater—you must think of the impact you want to create. Simplicity in a centerpiece can be clean and fresh, while a dramatic statement might strike a different chord. Sometimes you need a resting place, and other times it's all about being over the top. The centerpiece is one of my most cherished creative outlets when I set the table. I want to capture the essence of my vision for an evening or a breakfast or a tea. I know many people find an object that serves as the single, perfect centerpiece for a long time. I tend to like a fresh idea each time I set the table.

As long as I pack an open mind, with plenty of food for inspirational thought, I'm always ready to invent something new. Here are a few things I do to help myself dream up an original idea.

Collage:

To find just the right combination of objects, start by looking around your house. What are some of your favorite things, and what can you layer onto them to give your centerpiece a look that imitates collage? Usually a variety of heights and textures adds to the effect. Try using books, fabric remnants, an elegant vase, or votives. Just experiment by taking one layer at a time, and before you know it, you'll have mastered the art of creating impromptu centerpieces.

Color:

Finding inspiration in color can be an interesting way to approach your centerpiece. Perhaps you're looking at the shades of green in your dishes and pulling other objects into your table setting that are a similar shade of celadon, mint, or sage. On the flip side, a mosaic of different colors can create a centerpiece that is just as interesting with an entirely different spirit.

Journey Inspired:

A place you've visited or have always dreamed of can provide awesome inspiration for your table. Create a still life by assembling a few objects that remind you of a particular place. Ireland brings to mind the color green—sheep on rolling hills of pasture and creamy porcelain dishes. I brought these elements to my table with a sheet of moss, miniature ceramic sheep, and a small collection of teacups in lovely shades of cream. Your last trip to Ireland just inspired your table. Perhaps your memory takes you to tiny cottages with red roses climbing charming stucco walls. I love this approach because each person adds her own signature through her individual recollections.

Texture:

A friend of mine created a centerpiece inspired by objects with a tactile quality. For her still life, she set an ornately carved crystal cake plate; a lovely dove from her garden, made of rough, hardened plaster; a delicately brittle bird's nest filled with fluffy blue feathers, and then covered it all with a smooth, bell-shaped cloche. Around the cake stand were embossed candleholders set with sculptural ivory tapers that had been rolled in glitter to add sparkle to their raised patterns. A few votives were scattered at the base of the melange to add low, flickering light.

At Right: Inspired by the candles on a birthday cake, this centerpiece makes beautiful use of a damaged porcelain antique oil lamp. Inside, tulle (netting fabric) and glittered waxed paper hold the candles and tiny wax flowers in place. I love the way the tulle spills over the sides and creates an airy illusion of movement. A wreath of fresh greens and flowers surrounds the base. The look of this cocktail buffet is romantic and whimsical sitting on the Italian tapestry that my sister bought for me in Florence. Remember, your centerpiece can have some imperfections, which may make it as elegant as something perfectly neat and planned.

Below: I purchased this candle lantern to light up our barbecue for evening grilling. While the sparrows have adopted it as their springtime home, I still borrow it for a quick candlelit centerpiece once the baby birds have left. A row of small lanterns looks great on a long table, indoors or out. If you're lucky enough to discover several abandoned bird's nests, set them in a cluster and use them for pillar candles.

La lumière

candles

The image of a rustic campfire turns into pure elegance when burning logs are replaced with lit candles. Simple textural stones create a contrasting neutral base for scores of brightly colored candles. Centerpieces don't always have to exist on the table. Set one on a mantle or a chair, wherever you wish your guests' eyes to be drawn.

feathers

This year we decided to reinvent our Christmas decor. These oh, so ooh-la-la topiaries set the tone for a fabulous holiday season. This fine, feathered darling combines some traditional holiday elements (reindeer, cranberries, and glitter) with outrageous lavender feathers and delicious candy. We started with a foam topiary, an inexpensive white flocked deer, ribbons, feathers, candy, and cranberries. Think of all the things you can use from your ditzing kit to re-create them! Or simply use the base as is and change the top. Next season, perhaps you'll add a bouquet of springtime flowers.

flight

Tomato cages made from metal rods are really inexpensive and have an endless list of uses. Here we used ours to frame a kitschy still life of a flea-market garden print and a funky ceramic parrot statue. Our own hand-painted candleholders are tied with ribbon and perfectly finish the buffet, and, of course, it's okay that our candles and candleholders don't match.

Other outlandish tomato trellis uses:
- Wrap in tulle and use as you would a bulleti board—pin up quotes, photos, and inspiration for your soul.
- String with tea lights for a centerpiece with warm candlelit glow.
- During the holiday season, hang your most prized collection of ornaments as we did las year in our store.
- Put one inside an oversize vase to arrange extra long branches or flowers.

Here I wanted the table to become the focus of the party. This table is made by placing a wide wooden plank across twin garden urns and covering it with an area rug that's just back from the dry cleaner. I like to use my newly cleaned rugs as other coverings before they hit the floor for duty again.

When John and I were married, I made a gift for my mother-in-law-to-be and titled it *Mother Angel Bird*. This inexpensive angel was the inspiration for re-creating Margo's gift in three-dimensional form with layers of glittered flowers, vintage wallpaper, golden threads, and simple shells. The drama of the zebra rug was accented with scads of clear marbles, and all those flowering pots are her "garden." Perhaps the thought of someone you love will give life to your next centerpiece.

Challenge yourself! Our goal here was to pleasantly surprise ourselves with an idea that used bananas. They are layered with reindeer moss, which comes in a multitude of colors. A sprinkling of fake snow and candles nestled into the flower pots makes an unusual combination—pure decadence.

Make sure you look in every room for gems to enhance your centerpiece scheme. As I enter the bedroom, I can see that the Victorian beaded pillow and bird resting near my headboard would look great as the focal point on a table. Flirt with the inspirational!

The idea of creating miniature landscapes throughout the house intrigues me. I love this concept as a vignette in a glass cabinet, so I decided to try it to set off a table. I have many collections of animals, from miniature British antique lead pieces to flocked toys to colored plastic grocery-store trinkets. I pulled two of my flocked sheep from the collection and set them on their "pasture" of a pink pastel hat box. Easy to embellish with goodies, the sheep stand elegantly next to red cockscomb. The whole scene gets some height from a cake stand perch.

A fanciful tree grows up in style with lavender spray paint, feathers, and flowers. The resin angel is sprinkled with glitter and touches of paint.

Other ways to be inspired by trees:

- Have children in your life? Make them a real candy tree. Buy bags of pretty but inexpensive candy and start glueing.
- Little trees are darling for more than just Christmas. Pull them out on other holidays or festive occasions.
- A small "forest" of tiny trees would be a great idea for a tabletop landscape—maybe spray them in different shades of blue.
- Other things to perch little trees on: cake stands, paper-covered shoe boxes, a stack of antique plates, books.

handeliers make any space magical. In the studio and at home I am a bit obsessed with them. The girls are constantly reminding me how many I still have to hang just as I'm embarking on my latest purchase. I can't stop! They make me absolutely crazy, and the fact that they are so much fun to ditz makes them irresistible! This elegant creature was sprayed with adhesive and dusted with glitter. Next, we strung more crystals with metallic threads and added an extra layer of sparkle. Garlands of sheer ribbon drip from clusters of flocked birds and fanciful flowers. Looks good enough to eat!

I like to think of chandeliers as having many purposes (helps to justify the purchases, you know). In this case, it's not only a source of light and something to behold, but it's also the major centerpiece of a table. I have a particular chandelier in my dining room that hangs a bit closer to the table than most; the table has no choice but to take second place to its presence.

More goodies for ditzing your chandeliers:

- Fresh strawberries (your guests will delight in "picking" their own)
- Petit fours (perched or sitting on a base just below your crystals)
- Antique family photos
- Glittered feathers
- Hand-colored crystals (just use watercolor markers!). Most lamp supply stores carry a variety of crystals.
- Christmas ornaments
- Fresh herbs—lavender, mint, dill, scented geranium. Their aromas are lovely.
- Jewelry—new and old
- Dog biscuits, or any special treat appropriate for your pet's birthday

Check your ditzing kit list for more ideas!

It's all about scale! Branches, whether rustic, exotic, or flowering, can be cut in a variety of lengths. Imitations of our beloved peacock Zelda perch mischieviously in the trees. A centerpiece like this works on a buffet or centered on a table, and it will command a lot of attention. Look outside for more goodies to add, and ask yourself some questions. What's the look—simple and elegant, or inspired by lots of brilliant color? Try reds, oranges, and browns as a scheme. What extra something can you tie onto the branches? Explore . . . Explore . . . Explore . . .

Our Favorite Branches:
lilacs
forsythia
willow
pepper berries
vines of any kind
dogwood
cedar
locust
apple

87

THINK tiny; think demure. Little flowers in petite vases and old perfume bottles lined with tea lights. Exquisite reflections from the vintage mirror dance with candlelight.

Consider other tiny elements that will add detail to your piece: teacups, votives, coins, old keys, pretty stones, shells, leaves, and don't forget all those great dime-store treasures and fluff from your ditzing kit.

OVERWHELMING wonderfulness! A planter stacked with pillars makes quite a proclamation out of doors. Citrus fruits are bound with ribbon and tied with cheery bows. A lovely old bedspread in bright pink provides a textural contrast to the hard, metal stand.

THIS clear-glass cookie jar filled with colored sand, cacti, and candles becomes an eclectic centerpiece. Why not combine things from your home in unusual ways? It will set the tone, add intrigue, and be a great conversation piece at your next gathering.

STILL life as art. Pick a few of the favorite things in your environment and discover a way to create a centerpiece. I chose books, a favorite necklace, a framed butterfly, and my leopard scarf. Some basics to add scale or height to your still life: pitchers, vases, cake stands, pots, baskets, oversize candleholders.

Ah, the romance of Christmas. *Makes me want to dance in my dreams,* or am I flying? I can smell the savory scents—pine, a hint of mulling spices, and sweet cream. The fact is, I can taste it! Why, it's plump and sweet like sugarplums.

To me this room feels like an opera. It conjures up memories of walking through Versailles. I am overcome with a feeling of warmth and richness. The colors envelop me! There is the brilliance of fireflies, and it's magical! The holiday season is upon us—pure fantasy that sparkles like the inside of a fairy tale.

CHAPTER 9

The Holidays Are a Fine Romance

The holidays are a time for getting in touch with your past. I savor the process of setting it all up, planning get-togethers with friends. The rituals of cutting the boughs, dressing the window boxes, filling platters with luscious food, and decorating the house. Some years I spend hours in the kitchen surrounded by the smell of home-baked cookies; other years I'll take a whole weekend infusing the spirit of Christmas into the house. This year on my holiday break I spent two and a half days just wrapping presents. It felt like such a luxury to take that kind of time to do something I so enjoy. I'd go out to the studio and feel as if I was stealing some time alone there with my thermos of hot tea in tow. I'd light candles, and that vast, empty space never sounded so warm as it did filled with the sound of a beautiful opera. Change some of your holiday rituals from year to year; sprinkle in fantasy, but keep cherishing your traditions.

The essence of the holidays: chattering, laughter, the most splendid kind of chaos. Excitement that builds until you think you'll explode. Christmas morning, not being able to sleep, unthinkable to stay in bed any longer. Children drift in peaceful slumber, but in their dreams they wave their make-believe magic wands. They are romance in motion; in their heads, the ornaments on the tree sway in a waltz.

Remember yourself as a child. On your way home, you notice there is an unexplainable kick in your step, and the stars seem to shine a little brighter at this time of year. The romance of the holidays provides us with the greatest gift—memories. Cherish them and make some magic this year. Over the river and through the woods to Grandmother's house we go, past snow-covered driveways, until finally you arrive. The scene is candy dishes, an eternity of presents, and stockings hung with care. What's your favorite Christmas ritual? Make it last as long as you can.

Making Magic:
Reinventing a childhood
memory. My Grandma
Schaberg has always loved
angels, and it seemed that
every holiday someone in
the family would present
her with another for her
collection. This
chandelier was created
for the holidays in her
honor.

A garage-sale chandelier
was wrapped in baby blue ribbon and
pepper berry vines on the arms, while a lavender feather
boa hides an unsightly cord. The angel was covered in dainty flowers and
suspended with ropes of vine.

In Victorian times, the feather tree was typically surrounded by a miniature fence and used as a holiday center-piece. We decided to set ours on an antique plant stand to create a long, slender silhouette that complements lavender flocked paper.

Sweet

Deck the walls with boughs of holly, *fa la la la la la, la la la la la.* Create some theater with an already magnificent mirror. We made a gorgeous, bountiful wall hanging that can easily be moved. It displays the splendor of fruits, foliage, and vegetables any time of year.

Inspired to create your own?

- When selecting fruits and veggies, the harder the fruit and the thicker the skin, the longer it will last.

- We used brocoflower, lemons, oranges, artichokes, boxwood greens, holly berries, and leaves.

- For wall art that will last throughout the year, try using artificial elements.

- Are there other ways to bring fruit and veggies into your setting? How about piles of fruits and veggies arranged at the base of your tree? Strewn over a mantle?

Tidings

The pack rat strikes again! This cherub was salvaged from a damaged porcelain urn and now nestles on a bed of roses on our Christmas House.

The Christmas House is filled with tiny, fanciful scenes like this one. Create your own scene in a glass-fronted cabinet, and allow it to inspire your holiday window decorations next year.

Can you just imagine his wonderful sleigh? Enjoy classic ways to bring jolly old St. Nick into your holiday traditions using a flocked santa

- used as a napkin ring,
- perched on goblets,
- topping a Christmas gift,
- positioned on a centerpiece,
- sitting on the cookie tray.

I love creating little scenes. The image of children with visions of sugarplums dancing in their heads is about all that it took for us to get going on this one! If Santa Claus went to Candyland, this is where he'd live. We used a dollhouse on a table as the base and then created a wintery woodland with inexpensive miniature trees and fake snow spray. We used a variety of garlands from strands of beads to chenille roping to berry vines to flower garlands. Fill with goodies and sprinkle with fake snow.

Our Christmas House is meant to be just as much fun for adults as it is for kids. How about using it on top of a buffet to display desserts? Or setting up a Christmas House next year, instead of a Christmas tree? What a great place to store tiny gifts until the big day!

Ah . . . the fantasy is unveiled.

Putting all your effort into one room can make the outcome spectacular. If you'll be spending most of your time gathering with friends in a particular room, why not focus on it, instead of on the whole house? Remember to choose your battles wisely.

By focusing on one room, we can really pay attention to details: the walls, the tabletop, the floors. Consider the time of day you'll be entertaining—what kind of light will be available in the room? Playing with different heights, textures, and colors lets us imagine layers of lusciousness.

The table needed to be fabulous. We began with a grand centerpiece, something familiar but a tad unexpected. This fifty-dollar tree caught my eye, and I suddenly had a vision—Queen Elizabeth goes to Swan Lake.

Using a variety of inexpensive birds, we gave each its own unique personality—by the time we were done you'd think they could talk! Some were crowned with jeweled headdresses; others had rhinestone eyes that sparkled; crystals dangled from beaks; extra plumes were added for more elegant tails and others wore paper umbrella hats.

The tree was flocked with artificial snow and then layers of pink spray paint were applied. Vintage necklaces of baubles and beads were strung as garlands and the fanciful birds were perched upon the powdery branches.

This tree is such a beauty that she has now become a lovely centerpiece for our dining table in the studio. Additional birds were created to be used in other ways.

- Give birds as gifts to friends to celebrate the coming of spring.
- Decorate the top of a child's birthday cake.
- Attach them to a sconce or light fixture.

Wherever they land, they'll be a delight to behold.

Below Left: At the top of each feathered topiary is a mystical stag with glitter on his back and a crown of flowers in his antlers.

Even if you like to break the rules, it's fun to hang on to certain traditions. In my family, we have escargot every Christmas Eve. My grandma Lucy brought with her from France an elegant set of tiny pronged silver forks. Each year we make several dozen escargots using her delicious garlic-butter recipe. As we tuck each snail into the same shells that are now over seventy years old, we can't resist a moment to think of my Grandmother.

There is something sacred about guests taking their seats and exchanging intimate dinner conversation. I'm not sure I can put my finger on it exactly, but it seems to be about giving, receiving, and remembering.

So much glorious food. The sound of the oven door slamming, wooden spoons rapping on saucepans. These are familiar sounds—you know they mean the big day is here, time to take the apron off and get out of the kitchen. Feels like the first time you've sat down in weeks. All is prepared, and it's time to visit. Dishes are passed, glasses are filled, and stories are shared.

A Festive Menu:

1st Course:
escargot with lots of French bread to catch the extra garlic butter

2nd Course:
canapés, an assortment of tiny tastes

bowls and bowls of cured olives (lots of salties—
the next day we can barely bend our fingers)

dried salami, rosette de Lyon, and Soppressata

assorted cheeses—Asiago, Stilton, antique Gruyère, and Morbier

3rd Course:
pâté—liver is always a favorite

prosciutto-stuffed peppers

artichoke salad, savory with balsamic and rosemary

Main Course:
lobster tail grilled on a bed of tarragon and rosemary,
drizzled with a champagne butter sauce

Dessert Course:
petit fours

plum tartlettes

The holidays are about indulging yourself and others. Extravagance is a matter of taste: For some it's opening a rare vintage wine or using a luxurious cloth like velvet for napkins. Silver paper doily place mats were folded into a pouch embellished with two types of ribbon for texture, grosgrain and sheer organza, and finished with holly leaves and a tattered silk flower. Beside the velvet, this fancy handmade pouch holds a delicate trinket for each guest—a little something to remember an evening with friends or family.

Even a decorative mantle has a purpose when entertaining.

- *Set out champagne flutes before a special holiday toast.*

- *Serve your petite fours.*

- *Stash tiny gifts for guests.*

New Rituals

- Try on a different holiday color scheme—perhaps silver, mint green, and pink.
- Change your menu this year.
- Invite someone new to your family gathering.
- Adjust your gift routine. Try opening presents on Christmas Eve, or, if you already do, maybe on Christmas morning instead.
- Give only handmade gifts this year.
- Instead of making a phone call, send an invitation to family members for a holiday gathering.
- Get dressed up on Christmas Day. Or don't, if you usually do.
- Dim the lights, turn off the television, and light the candles.
- Take your time, have a sip of sherry, and make a festive toast!

Magical Words

- Glisten. Makes me think of snow, crystals, glitter. Perhaps these words inspire me to decorate my table with costume jewelry and to add glass elements to my centerpiece, or use glitter on my place cards.
- Dream. Makes me think of a holiday wish. Perhaps one wish for every person at the table, and I'll write it next to their name on the place card. A tiny, but thoughtful offering.
- Enchanted. Reminds me of the children who will be present at our table—perhaps an inexpensive treat is on each of their plates.

Old Traditions

- Send handwritten Christmas cards.
- String popcorn.
- Make a batch of eggnog.
- Spend an afternoon Christmas caroling.
- Light a candle and take a walk in the snow.
- Leave cookies and hot cocoa out for Santa.
- Set up a train around the tree.
- Hang mistletoe.
- Decorate a wreath for the front door.
- Pull out your ice skates.
- Go sledding.
- Roast chestnuts.
- Bake Christmas cookies.
- Cut down your own tree.
- Keep your decorations up from Thanksgiving to New Year's Day.

Holiday Entertaining Checklist

- Champagne in the fridge
- Five new Christmas CDs
- Extra presents wrapped for unexpected guests
- Plenty of candles
- An assortment of candy—great for stuffing stockings and filling candy dishes
- Fresh fruit, crackers, and cheese for impromptu holiday visitors
- Lots of gift wrap, tape, ribbon, boxes, and tags for presents
- Cocktail napkins
- Film—think about videotape too!
- Greens (Order in early November or plan a day to forage.)
- Christmas gift bags for holiday favors of home-baked goods

Pinwheels and Pixie Sticks—as kids we were tickled pink to get either! But the idea of two in one is darling. Add a few bells and whistles to your pinwheel. Here we used a velvet pansy and some bits of acetate ribbon cut into tails. Finish with a fun gift tag, and you're ready to pass the magic wand to friends, young and old. A delightful treat for the hostess's children and an inexpensive party favor for friends and family.

Goodies, gifts, and more goodies—love to give 'em, love to get 'em. I like to get creative with gifts so they become less material, more a reminder of the gathering. Some of the most precious gifts are those given and received with a sense of humor. A heartfelt note or a handmade present speaks volumes to the soul. Remember, this is not about making yourself crazy—if you don't have the time, the heck with it. When you want to keep it simple, use the same theme as your event to make gifts and favors. A reminder of the evening will touch all of those near and dear to you.

Where do the gifts go? At each guest's place at the table, or in a basket or container offered when everyone arrives or leaves. Perhaps use your gifts to fill the bathtub, where most guests will make a trip at some point during their visit. How about attached to or inside of the centerpiece? A neat way to revisit a wonderful gathering is to send handmade photo albums several weeks after the event.

I once attended a dinner where Asian and Japanese foods were served, and each guest was presented with a mysterious silver box by our hostess. When the boxes were opened, they each revealed six pieces of hand-rolled sushi and a fortune typed on parchment paper. Each guest read their fortune aloud and accepted the words of wisdom as the evening's token. A simple gesture, yet memorable.

Our fabric-covered box was filled with reindeer moss (craft supply stores sell it by the bag and in a rainbow of colors). Tuck some artificial flower blooms in between the fruits. For a handmade look, decoupage the lid of the box with pages of an international newspaper.

Je t'aime les Surprises

Snow globes make me a little bit crazy! I mean, really, all that glitter, fake snow, the miniature scenes, yummy stuff floating around in water—it's enough to make anyone nuts! The fact that I can't get to all those treats inside is maddening. So, this gift gives the illusion of a snow globe while still letting the recipient get to the goods.

A Tracy Diversion: I vividly recall a kindergarten classmate inviting me to her birthday party where someone gave her a shoe box filled with this kind of deliciousness! I can still picture all the stuff: lollipops, plastic animals, different kinds of candies, toys, party favors, stickers, and bubble gum. I remember thinking about how much I'd like to receive a present like that.

In my classmate's honor, we present to you the snow globe jar, chock-full o' goodies:

- Take any flea market jar or glass storage container with a removable lid. Decorate the lid's edge with rickrack, trim, or ribbon. Use tiny fabric flowers to create a bed of roses, and then hot-glue your goodies to the top. Fill the jar with the most fun things you can think of, and you are good to go! Fantastic for birthdays, graduations, or any celebration. A mini version makes a great party favor—try a baby food jar for this concept.

- Get the idea? Create a list of what you might put inside a jar for an artist, writer, gardener, or a sweetheart.

Stumped for a wedding shower favor or a hostess gift? Try this little pretty: A small, tin box daintily holds an antique spoon, darling sugar cubes, and a sachet of loose tea, elegantly wrapped in tulle and tied with a lavender satin ribbon.

- For coffee lovers—substitute coffee beans for tea.
- For children—substitute a packet of Kool-Aid for tea.
- For a sick friend—try packets of soup, lozenges, and vitamin C tablets.

A simple favor to feed the soul. A cellophane bag holds a fortune cookie with a secret message, a charm, and a single chocolate wrapped as a gold coin. You can find foil-wrapped candies on grocery shelves in piles during the holidays. Stock up while you can.

This a fabulous favor for a treasure-hunt party, or when your menu leans toward the exotic. Label each bag with the name of a guest and the favor doubles as a place card for the table.

I dream in layers of baby blue velvet. When you wrap, have some options on hand.

- Think unconventional paper— wallpaper, florist foil, tissue paper, craft paper, sheet moss.
- The top of the present is easy to create when your stash is stocked.
- For a baby gift, work with candy, animal crackers, and antique baby booties.
- For anytime, use glittered fruits and flowers, vintage jewelry, pressed leaves, sequins, plastic toys, and Matchbox cars.

My dear friend Sarah knows that I'm obsessed with new, fresh towels. I incessantly repeat how much I love to look at a new stack of towels and she fulfilled my wishes with this gift of new kitchen linens. Knowing my pack-rat mentality, Sarah knows that the ribbons and crystals will be reused on chandeliers and that the vintage bracelet will make its way to my dining table as a napkin ring.

Other sets any hostess would like to have on hand: a set of napkins, taper candles, some pretty notepaper, a set of silver teaspoons, or a bouquet of fresh flowers.

These handmade key chains are a thoughtful way to send to friends the message that you'd like to entertain them for a spell. Not using the cottage this month? Send keys to a friend who could use some time away from the city.

Abandoning the city apartment for a sabbatical? Perhaps your nephew might like some time away from the folks.

- Charms, tags, string, photo corners, clips, stickers, decoratively cut card stock, ribbons, plastic toys, and crystals are combined to create this assortment of flirty ideas. Tie these pretties to a present for a whimsical gift tag.

Sweets for the sweet. A cookie decorated with icing makes a special treat. Place it in a cellophane bag and hot-glue an antique button and a scrap of beaded trim to embellish the package. When you compose the message, give the gathering a title, such as: "First of many starry nights at the cabin." Include the date, guest list, and menu as a memento of the evening.

Message on the bottle. The classic hostess gift doesn't have to be predictable. A simple touch goes a long way.

I believe that you can never have too many candles. Any time is right for giving and receiving more candlelight. Candles make wonderful hostess gifts or party favors. A floral antique saucer makes a charming base for now, and a darling soap dish later. Pastel buttons are secured to the candle with hot glue, and a note and matchsticks are tied up with twine.

Let the box inspire the wrap. This tattered hatbox gets dressed up with paper doll dresses, rhinestones, buttons, antique pins, millinery flowers, and more! Saucy fringe and pleated ribbon skirt the lid, while an antique postcard recalls a sentimental message.

Out of boxes? How about some of these: empty paint cans, baskets, cigar boxes, oversize jars, lunch boxes, old tins, and pie pans.

Fresh picked from your yard or garden. When you're in a hurry, there's nothing better than reaching for what's outside your door. This asparagus gets a pretty ribbon, fabric leaves, and a sugared berry.

How about berries from the vine? A charming bowl tied with ribbon is a refreshing summer treat.

What's out there anyway? Have you looked lately?

- Flowers? Romantically nestled in a sweep of pastel tissue paper.
- Wheat? Tied with elegant wired ribbon, it will look great on a mantle.
- Flowering branches? Long and sprawling, these will make a stunning arrangement.
- Twigs? Tied up with dried citrus, cinnamon sticks, and cedar.
- Kale? Tucked into flower blossoms.
- Fruits? Settled into a bird's nest.

A creative soul can't resist the temptation of giving the gift of beauty.

guest journal

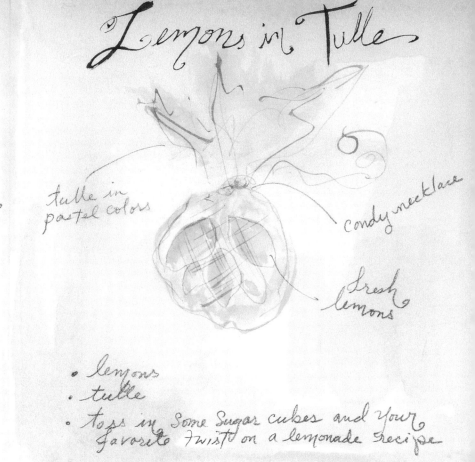

photo of you and
your friends

a couple of
lucky pencils

parlez-vous français?

ribbons

- A blank Journal
- Your favorite memory of
  their home
- tie up with String and good Wishes

Lemons in Tulle

tulle in
pastel colors

candy necklace

fresh
lemons

- lemons
- tulle
- toss in some sugar cubes and your
  favorite twist on a lemonade recipe

Wine in Wallpaper

glitter

ribbons

favorite
wine or
bubbly

antique or
new Wallpaper

flowers or
Treasures

- there are only a billion other things
  you could wrap this in
- Must glitter the top!

Horn of Plenty

Bon
Bons

Easter grass

ribbons

- make a cone of anything you desire
- fill with goodies
- put a secret fortune inside bottom

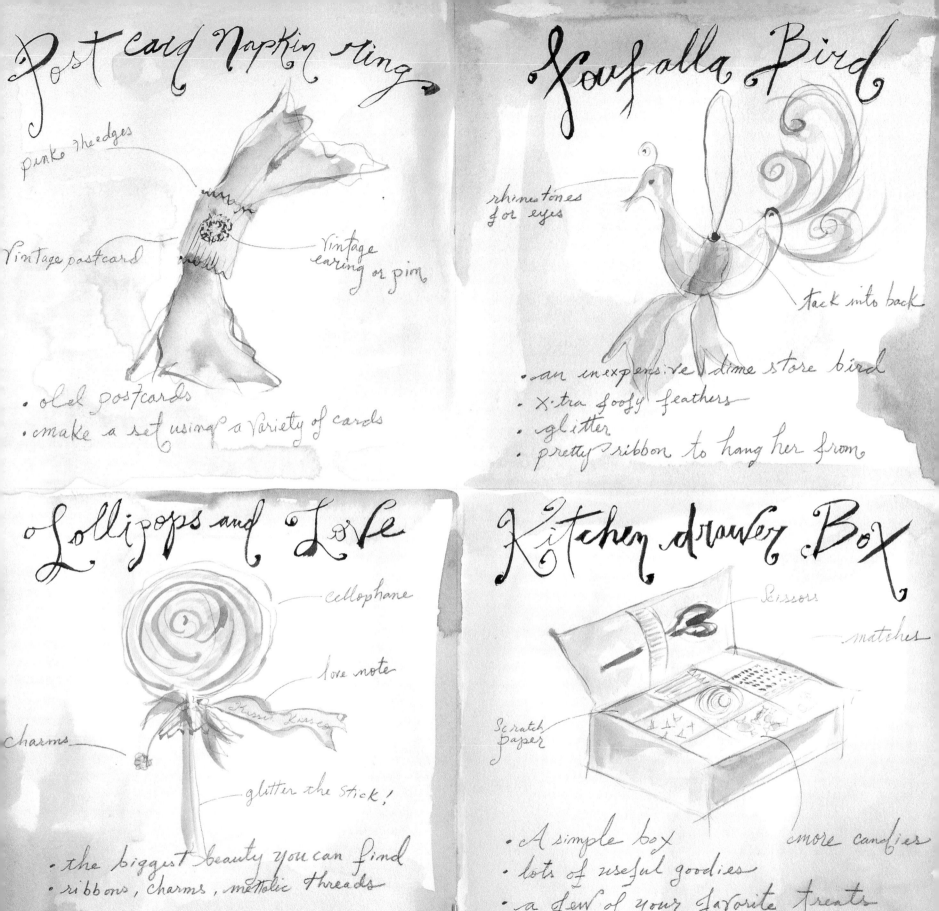

Post card Napkin ring

pink theedges

Vintage postcard

Vintage earing or pim

- old postcards
- make a set using a variety of cards

Soufalla Bird

rhinestones for eyes

tack into back

- an inexpensive dime store bird
- x-tra goofy feathers
- glitter
- pretty ribbon to hang her from

Lollizops and Love

cellophane

love note

Kisses Kisses

charms

glitter the stick!

- the biggest beauty you can find
- ribbons, charms, mettalic threads
- Kisses xoxo

Kitchen drawer Box

Scissors

matches

Scratch paper

- A simple box   more candies
- lots of useful goodies
- a few of your favorite treats

Most people I know, whether city or country dwellers, get a kick out of a change of scenery. And who doesn't love grabbing a bit of the outdoors for a while? Taking advantage of the warm weather months is so essential. Dining alfresco can mean more than filling a wicker hamper with sandwiches and spreading a checked cloth. Next time, try a little fantasy, too.

CHAPTER 11

Leftovers and Lazy Afternoons

The idea of reinventing the outdoor dining experience came to us in September, just at the end of a long Indian summer. My friend Sarah and I came up with a plan for spending a fall afternoon with the guys out on our marsh. A little intrigue is always good, so we decided that our excursion would be a surprise. Our idea was to spend some time out on the marsh in a canoe, take an evening hike, plant ourselves at our version of a campsite and enjoy a relaxing meal.

Keep in mind other natural places you can experience: a park; your backyard; a forest preserve; a meadow; a nearby riverbank, lake, or pond.

We borrowed a friend's canoe and sneaked it to the site a few days ahead of time.

A week before our outing, Matt and John each happened upon a fanciful cornucopia filled with treats. The guys peeked inside to find a mysterious message handwritten on the Queen of Hearts:

September 17, 4:00 P.M.
Meet us at the Porters' marsh
xoxo, S and T

Boxed lunches take on a whole new meaning here. Instead of serving right from the Colonel's bucket, we covered basic shoe boxes in a variety of textures from wrapping paper to vintage wallpaper. We lined the interiors loosely with waxed paper, and embellished lids with craft store birds, acorns, berries, twigs, and leaves; then placed lunch inside. No doubt these charmers will be used again and again. You could also use them to give a gift to a friend or to store lingerie, tissue, or cosmetics.

~Our Menu~
Cold Fried Chicken
Broccoli Coleslaw
Corn Muffins
Honey Butter
Red Potato Salad
Lemon Bars

We had to find creative ways to get our goods to the campsite. Here, luncheon plates got tied with leather shoelaces.

What can you use instead of a picnic basket to tote your goods to an outdoor adventure?

A wheelbarrow, a laundry sack, a child's wagon, an old pillowcase, a child's lunch box, a backpack. For a winter outing? Try pulling your stuff on a sled.

Since we knew that setting up an environment outdoors would take some effort, we quickly decided to simplify the food detail by picking up a bucket of chicken and spicing up some leftovers. I like having my fun and taking things over the top, but I'm definitely not interested in spending all my free time making myself crazy. My philosophy: How can I make it special without making myself insane? The minute an event becomes an ordeal or guilt is involved, you're no longer enjoying your journey.

We planned a simple menu based on what we each had on hand. Sometimes one substitution or the addition of an ingredient can add a whole new dimension to a menu. Here are a few of our innovations:

- Try adding a jar of apricot preserves or candied ginger into corn muffin batter.
- Instead of honey, use a food processor to whip one of the following into butter: pickled jalapeño, maple syrup, brown sugar and cinnamon, roasted garlic, or red peppers.

Potato salad is an American tradition. Give yours a little twist with Kalamata olives, capers, roasted red pepper, sun-dried tomato chutney, or spicy brown mustard.

For those in search of the perfect lemon bar . . .

Crust: must be at least one-quarter inch thick

Taste: that perfect balance of sweet and sour

Top: must have thin layer of powdered sugar

Serve: with edible flowers as garnish—
(viola shown here)

Best when eaten the day after

There is a wonderful spot on our property where a rickety old porch swing hangs from one of many magnificent oaks near the quarry and the marsh. Drawing inspiration from my memory of childhood campsites and the tents we made from old blankets "borrowed" from Mom's linen closet, I rig a fantasy tent out of inexpensive tulle.

Old-fashioned pastimes like rowing a canoe or hiking a trail are still some of the best ways to have casual gatherings with friends. In the country, we sometimes take for granted the simple rituals of sharing with others. But it's probably those weekend visits with friends from the city that remind us just how lucky we are that some of these simple traditions remain.

When is the last time you did the following:

- Went to an orchard to pick fruit?
- Found an old-fashioned soda fountain and had an ice-cream sundae?
- Were tempted by the abundance of a roadside stand?
- Took pride in selecting your own pumpkin from the patch?
- Went into the woods to cut down your own Christmas tree?
- Ate a burger at a joint where you sat in your car and got served by a waitress on skates?
- Watched a movie through the front window of your car?
- Visited a county fair?

We picked our own Buttercup design as the dish of choice, inspired by casual afternoons filled with cheery sunshine. Whimsical paper cups are tied with a sheer organza ribbon bow and stamped with hot-wax seals. Fried chicken gets messy, so not one but two paper napkins are wrapped with a dragonfly around tag-sale flatware.

The shoreline around the marsh is thick with stone and rock, so we pass on the picnic blanket and lay our spread on a comfy wool hooked rug instead. We call this design Artesian—named after the road I lived on when I was growing up.

A token reminder of the day's events is the gift of a photo frame made with elements found in nature.

With food and gifts under control, we're free to put our heads toward our favorite task of setting the stage. There is no table to hold a flower arrangement or centerpiece, but in her earnest desire to hang on to the final days of a fading summer garden, Sarah makes a breathtaking floral masterpiece. We suspend her creation of cascading blooms from the center of our tulle tent and call it the flowering chandelier.

Sarah puts a fistful of flowers and vines from her garden into a florist's foam ball, then fastens a loop of fine-gauge wire around the ball of the chandelier for hanging. Think of this beauty hung indoors, or as a centerpiece resting in a nest of grapevine. Or use smaller florist foam balls to create several miniature versions and mix them into the table setting.

It is officially autumn, but at dusk the air is still warm. We won't need the hot blaze of a wood fire this evening. Instead, we create a campfire using candles and primitive-looking stones. The ritual of sitting in candlelight is an indulgence that John and I gratefully take every evening. But it is such an overwhelming experience to sit under the stars with candles twinkling and watch the fall of night with dear friends.

123

Why not create a fanciful centerpiece? A flocked deer becomes the main character in a surreal wonderland scene. He stands in a bed of reindeer moss and flowers, surrounded by a ring of leaves. An elegant garland of paper flowers and millinery leaves hangs from his neck in a mélange of texture. Covered with a cloche, it's like peeking into a looking glass.

CHAPTER 12

Beyond Posies

*N*ot sure how to let nature enhance your entertaining? In an arrangement, you can get almost any effect from demure to obscure. But don't stop there, think beyond vessels and urns. Explore other ways to infuse the beauty of nature into your entertaining experience.

- Add a pretty layer to a dessert tray with mint leaves.
- Create brilliant colors in soup, ice cubes, and scones by adding edible flowers.
- Use a maple leaf as a distinctive coaster.
- Drop plump raspberries into ginger ale.
- Experiment with a landscape of nature on your tabletop.
- Make a charming charger for a luncheon plate wth a lily pad.
- Dazzle your guests with a centerpiece of gold fish swimming in a hand-painted bowl.
- Deck out your lamp shades with a "fringe" trim of vine and berries.
- Spray a pillar candle with adhesive and roll in it dried herbs— sensual scents of lavender, rosemary, and sage.
- Create a grapevine table runner woven with feathers, ribbons, vines, berries, and moss.
- Sprinkle sugared rose petals in a cup of tea.

Pack an open mind when you play with nature.

I don't know how something will come together until I'm in the middle of it. Many times I surprise myself with a "happy" accident; the unintentional is better than anything I could have dreamed up in my head. When playing with nature's elements, your next mistake just might astound you.

This was a papier-mâché dragonfly from the craft store. We dirtied up his wings and dusted them with glitter for a gossamer effect, added silk leaves and a millinery flower from a vintage hat. Voilà! A bud vase becomes a gift for all at our last family picnic.

At Right: Fruit Salad with a twist!
This mini watermelon becomes the perfect vase for a summer garden party. The flower stems are held in a hole cut into the top of the sweet stuff, and the fruit holds enough water to keep the flowers happy for days.
What other ways can fruits be used with flowers?
Limes stacked inside a clear vase with tulips spilling out of the top.
Clumps of ripe grapes dripping over the edge of a pretty pitcher.
Just add water and a bouquet of flowers.
Cranberries floating in a glass vase of long-stemmed flowers.
Everyone loves sweet and sour.

This cement block goes from austere to sensational with flowering herbs and branches. Slices of kiwi are tucked into this indoor/outdoor (better use your umbrella) arrangement. What other ordinary containers can you turn into fabulous planters or vases?

- chipped old soup tureen
- ceramic pitcher
- an antique dresser drawer

This old milk bottle carrier makes a great gathering basket in the garden. This morning's offering was so beautiful, I couldn't help myself—I had to add food coloring to the water. Gracing my front step, these simple jars will be enjoyed by all who come to visit.

Every woman needs to feel like a princess, so why not create a silk slipper? We tucked flowers and rhinestones into the toe and tied it up with organdy tendrils. Dress up a silver tray by placing this lovely on it as you serve tea and cookies to friends. I was inspired by my mother-in-law, who used her grandmother's wedding shoes as the centerpiece for Nana's (John's grandmother) birthday a few years ago.

Flowers don't always have to be put into containers and vases. Strung from up above, this floral chandelier makes a wonderful focal point above the table or in a doorway. A florist foam ball was soaked in water to keep flower stems moist, and then was covered with some of the last blooms of this summer's garden. Create pure magic outside by hanging from an outdoor canopy or the branch of a tree.

Think outside of the vase. Here, fruits and flowers are arranged beside a pretty pitcher in a sunny windowsill. I picked a colored crystal pitcher that looks magnificent in the sun.

The true beauty of glass and beaded flowers is that they glisten forever. These lovelies grace my home all year long, especially in February when it's slim pickings in Wisconsin for fresh-cut flowers. I cherish this porcelain Staffordshire vase which was a birthday present from Mom and Dad.

Before a gathering, I can be found out on the property at Stonehouse Farm looking for fruits, flowers, and branches to pull into my party environment. On each excursion, I'm amazed at what I find. I'm constantly surprised from one harvest to the next, never knowing what I'll come up with. But believe me when I tell you—*the sky's the limit.*

Surprise yourself—you don't need a farm to take a foraging journey.

How about any of these:

- the grassy area on the side of the road
- your mother's garden
- a window box (can be found in the city or the country)
- your neighbor's lilac bush (don't forget to ask before you indulge)

A bouquet of apple branches, cattails, and wild vines can be as charming and elegant as store-bought flowers. Remember, it's not about perfection or spending money, it's about color, texture, and your imagination. Have fun!

I call this my *"rat's nest"* bouquet. An abundance of anything can make an impact. Play a game—force yourself to create an arrangement with the first two things that catch your eye on the hunt. An easy way is to create an unlikely combination—a host of oak-leaf branches meets an assault of wild asters. Think of the statement this will make when discovered indoors!

Try these on:

- wheat
- grapevines
- tall grasses
- red willow branches

Beyond posies to a floral wallpaper border from our collection. Add as a decorative edge to a table, wrap around the bottom of a glass or the base of a cake plate.

Tansy and dried button flowers make the perfect bonnet for this lemon. Tied with sheer ribbon, these little beauties could sweeten anything:

- Think decorating a chandelier
- Think hanging from a tall centerpiece
- Think creating a candelabra
- Think embellishing a napkin ring
- Think beautifying the arm of each dining chair

Milk pods and cedar branches fill this decorative urn. The floral foam inside is hidden with reindeer moss. This will be perfectly at home on top of the mantle or anywhere that needs some height and easy shape.

We talk a lot about "recycling" objects and reaching outside of the ordinary to find sources of inspiration. This fancy tree is a great example—a mosaic wastepaper basket becomes the "stand." The tree cone is made of grapevine. Fuchsia-dyed branches of leaves (from the flower shop) are wired onto the cone and then heather is used to fill in sparse areas. Tea light candles are nestled to create a magical tree—gorgeous day or night.

(Right to Left)

Hypericum

Myrtle

Flowering Eucalyptus

Dyed Integrafolia

Podocarpus

Rosehips

Willow Eucalyptus

Pepperberry

Tope

Euphorbia (Snow on the Mountain)

Camillea Foliage

Seeded Eucalyptus

Diosma

Mount Breesia Pod

Tansy

Hypericum

Campanula

You can truly find a way to use anything! At the studio, we tend to use any natural resource that grows here on the farm. When we've just got to have something that doesn't, we enlist the help of nurseries and flower shops. It's all about variety and knowing what our needs are: Sometimes we want color, a fleshy petal, the particular shape of a leaf, or a sprig of berries. The greenery is just as important as the flowers and fruits.

Sometimes simple is the best. I used this old milk glass citrus juicer as a bowl for floating a few flower blossoms. Perfect for in a powder room or in the bedroom of visiting guests.

A great way to dress an artificial Christmas wreath for a springtime party. Florist foam is soaked in water and attached to the back of the wreath. Give any of your evergreen decorations a wake-up call! We added everything from leaves to flowers to fresh lemon slices. A framed collection of butterflies is nestled into the center.

I call this "the lemon drop." *Can you tell that candy really does rule my world!* My entryway lantern greets our visitors day and night. When lit, a candle in the center of a glass vessel shines through lemon slices.

With all of this inspiration around me, I'm constantly trying to think of new ways to use nature while I'm changing the house or setting the table for friends.

Here are some ideas that add a twist to the traditional:

- Christmas Garland/*Garland of flowers*
- Basket of Flowers/*Basket made of flowers*
- Corsage/*Corsage as napkin holder*
- Paper Flowers/*Flowers used as paper*

After a wild week, it's time to unwind and catch a few "girlfriend" moments away from the studio with a cocktail.

CHAPTER 13

City in the Country

I thrive on the here and now we live in—it's all about instant gratification and having some of all of it. Every day we find more ways to get information a little faster, and for many of us the pace of our lives seems to be picking up speed. Downtime with friends and family is more precious than ever. We all have times when life gets a bit out of control, and an impromptu occasion is just the thing when you're especially pressed for time. Keep it simple; sometimes you just need to make a gathering quick and easy.

We all know the drill:

- Get friends together during the week after everyone, including you, has had a long day at work?
- You're cramming for a deadline, but need a few hours with family to rejuvenate?
- You don't have time, but you want to do something nice for someone whose life is in transition ?
- A dream home building project has, for the moment, turned a family upside down?

Whatever the situation is, I hope some of the ideas in this chapter make your impromptu occasions go more smoothly. Or at the very least, they'll remind you to enjoy the journey.

Shish kebobs! I'm not sure what the word means or where it comes from, but I know that when you're in a hurry, they are brilliantly easy! Talk about instant gratification, these are all about jamming the best foodstuffs you can find onto a skewer and cooking over an open fire.

We all know the classic ingredients for shish kebobs, but once in a while go for entirely new delectables!

The combination is the thing that makes a shish kebob. Here's my fantasy list of ingredients:

- lobster
- mango
- fennel
- plums
- Greek olives
- pea pods
- lamb
- Gruyère cheese wrapped in spinach
- bread dipped in olive oil and balsamic vinegar
- baby artichokes

Just the right time to pull out the disposables—remember this is about quick and easy. Paper forks, paper plates used naked (no glitter, jewels, or feathers), and paper napkins are in perfect order. (We couldn't resist a plastic toy and a little ribbon.)

Our friends Christine Phillips and John Castino toast to the end of an ambitious week!

Can't compromise on the cocktails! John makes his concoction of the moment—The Ultimate Bloody Mary.

To be armed and ready have the following ingredients on hand:

- Clamato
- vodka
- Dijon mustard
- Tabasco
- Worcestershire sauce
- horseradish
- juice from any jar of pickled veggies
- lime juice
- lemon pepper seasoning
- celery salt
- garnish: celery, lime, olives, cherry tomatoes, baby corn, pickled okra, brussel sprouts, mushrooms (or any other veggie that comes pickled)!

Serve a Bloody Mary in a martini glass?
Sure, why not? Each gets a tie-dyed ribbon and a sprig of wired rhinestones.

Cocktail skewers can be fun—how about trying hat pins or embellishing the top of a toothpick skewer? The longer the skewer, the more goodies you get.

More ideas for impromptu occasions:

- Forget setting the table for a sit-down dinner. Let guests mingle with appetizers served from a buffet.
- Soup—it's your best bet for easy clean up, a one-bowl meal!

John calls his sister "One-Pot-Annie" because she loves making casseroles. I think she's got just the right formula for comfort food with no fuss and no mess.

- When you can't take the time to cook, order in or carry out!
- Eat a meal at your coffee table.
- Have your friends over. Put jammies on and watch a video from your bed.
- Order a pizza and "doctor" it up with your own pantry full of yummies! Try roasted garlic chutney, feta cheese with fried ham and pineapple, sauerkraut, hot peppers.
- Serve breakfast foods, which tend to be quick and easy— how about having friends over for a pancake dinner? Don't forget an extra capful of vanilla in your batter.
- Prepare a trio of popcorn:
  Lemon pepper and grated Parmesan cheese
  Maple syrup tossed with a crumbled Heath candy bar
  Tabasco sauce and melted cheddar cheese

Need an extra table for an impromptu buffet? A friend of mine improvised by throwing an old door over two sawhorses.

- Line up a few folding tables and cover with an inexpensive, printed bed sheet.
- Add wheels to a table made of inexpensive lumber, and your serving station goes mobile.

On the following pages, our precious desserts—made to order for the impromptu occasion!

Impromptu Deliciousness

Vanilla Mule

·1·

Amelia's Breakfast

·2·

Sur la Pont

·3·

dream A little dream

·4·

Hats of Yum

·5·

Midnight Blankie

·6·

The How and Why

1

- The richest Vanilla ice cream

- Warm peanut butter drizzled over it

- Sprinkled with chopped mango's, bananas and crushed sugar ice cream cones

What more does a girl need.... (this or a new pair of shoes!)

2

My cat Amelia's favorite petite déjeuner

• Your loveliest spoons dipped in white chocolate... cool it baby!

• Fresh raspberries...... sitting in a pool of warm cream .... in which you've melted shaved white chocolate till thickened.....

3

I'd jump from a bridge to dive into this!

• Toasted and buttered (sweet cream....) pound cake from the grocery store... covered in coconut tapioca ..... make it by substituting ⅓ of milk with coconut milk .....

4

Poached bartlett pears ...... drizzeled with maple cream. .... (take caramels and melt with maple syrup and cream cheese) .....

If you close your eyes you can taste it .....

5

Puff pastry shells..... find in the freezer dept. @ your grocery store .....

Fill these little gems with anything that makes you sing .....

Puddings, creams, cobblers, sorbets ... la, la, la, la, la ....

6

Most decadent hot chocolate ....

half milk half cream with shaved chocolate bars and white chocolate slowly melted in ..... oooh...

and then a major dollop of coffee ice cream plunked in .....

serve with favorite cookies from your youth ....

good night!